# Designing Effective Early Childhood Environments

Anne Cairns Federlein, Ph.D.
State University College at Oneonta
Oneonta, New York

Cynthia A. Puls, Director
City of Southfield Employee Child Care Center
Southfield, Michigan

Judith M. Finkelstein, Ph.D.
University of Northern Iowa
Cedar Falls, Iowa

*Photographs by April S. Haase*
*Drawings by Donald Root*

KENDALL/HUNT PUBLISHING COMPANY
4050 Westmark Drive   Dubuque, Iowa 52002

This edition has been printed directly from camera-ready copy.

Copyright © 1994 by Kendall/Hunt Publishing Company

ISBN 0-8403-9199-4

All rights reserved. No part of this publication may be reproduced, stored in a retrieval system, or transmitted, in any form or by any means, electronic, mechanical, photocopying, recording, or otherwise, without the prior written permission of the copyright owner.

Printed in the United States of America
10  9  8  7  6  5  4  3  2  1

"Play teaches children to master the world."

Jean Piaget (1896-1980)

Photo copyright April S. Haase

Photo copyright April S. Haase

# Contents

ACKNOWLEDGEMENT ............................................................................... IX

INTRODUCTION ........................................................................................ XI
Ecology of Early Childhood Classrooms ................................................... XI

CHAPTER I ................................................................................................... 3
PHYSICAL ENVIRONMENT AFFECTS LEARNING
Physical Environment Affects Learning ..................................................... 3
A Learning Environment ............................................................................. 3
Importance of Movement ............................................................................ 5
Relating to Others ........................................................................................ 6
Importance of Play ...................................................................................... 6
Role of the Teacher ..................................................................................... 7
Primary Classrooms .................................................................................... 8
Teaching Cooperation ................................................................................. 9
Questions for Chapter I ............................................................................. 11

CHAPTER II ............................................................................................... 15
PROMOTING MOVEMENT IN EARLY CHILDHOOD ENVIRONMENTS
Movement is Necessary ............................................................................. 15
Development of Language, Social Skills and Cognition ......................... 16
Associations Learned ................................................................................ 17
Blocks, Blocks, Blocks .............................................................................. 18
Questions for Chapter II ........................................................................... 20

CHAPTER III .............................................................................................. 23
DESIGNING EARLY CHILDHOOD CLASSROOMS
Environment Has Two Elements .............................................................. 23
Basic Requirements ................................................................................... 23
Size of the Classroom ................................................................................ 24
Number of Children .................................................................................. 25
Storage Units ............................................................................................. 25
Evaluation of Equipment and Materials ................................................... 26
Equipment .................................................................................................. 26
Materials .................................................................................................... 27
Structuring Paths Between Centers .......................................................... 27
Dimensions to Include in Designing a Classroom ................................... 28
Designing Curricular Centers ................................................................... 29
Summary .................................................................................................... 32
Questions for Chapter III .......................................................................... 34

**CHAPTER IV** ............................................................................................... 35
**DEVELOPING THE CURRICULUM**
Role of the Teacher ........................................................................................ 38
Role of the Administrator ............................................................................... 39
Different Kinds of Play .................................................................................. 39
Children's Needs ............................................................................................ 40
Guidelines for Purchasing Materials .............................................................. 41
Physical Environment .................................................................................... 43
Outdoor Area .................................................................................................. 44
Program Evaluation ........................................................................................ 45
Questions for Chapter IV ............................................................................... 46

**CHAPTER V** ................................................................................................ 47
**SUGGESTED EQUIPMENT FOR EARLY CHILDHOOD ENVIRONMENTS**
Equipment to Construct for Early Childhood Environments ........................ 49
Early Childhood Classroom Equipment ........................................................ 49
Room Arrangements for Preschools and Kindergartens ............................... 98
Room Arrangements for Primary Grades .................................................... 106

**BIBLIOGRAPHY** ...................................................................................... 115

**RESOURCES** ............................................................................................ 121

**PUBLICATION RESOURCES** ................................................................ 122

**RESOURCE ORGANIZATIONS** ............................................................ 125

**ACKNOWLEDGMENT**

To our families and colleagues

To those who made a difference and inspired us to live our lives as early childhood professionals, and to our former students who are now our colleagues. A special acknowledgement is given to April S. Haase who so expertly captured the spirit of our children on film in this text, as well as in *An Introduction to the Business of Child Care*.

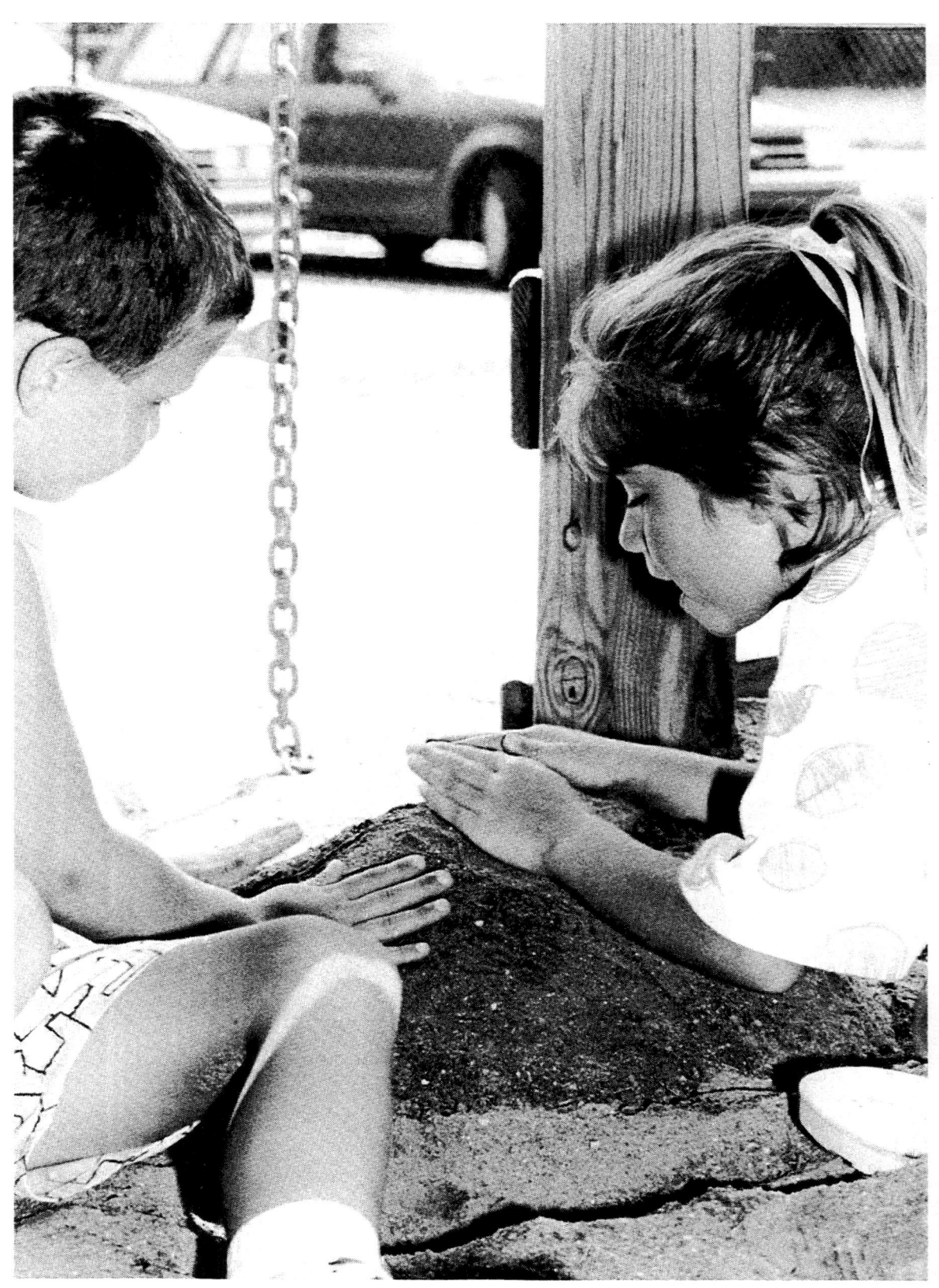

Photo copyright April S. Haase

# INTRODUCTION

**Ecology of Early Childhood Classrooms**

What equipment is needed to facilitate learning in an early childhood environment? Young children who are successfully challenged in the area of motor development also develop social skills and self esteem on physical equipment. As in the curriculum, good equipment encourages curiosity and promotes problem solving, decision making and creative thinking.

All early childhood classrooms have different physical layouts, but must meet the needs of young children. Creative use of space continues to be of interest to early childhood professionals because children are now in child care centers and classrooms for longer periods of time than ever before in our history.

We are just discovering the need for getaway places in a home-like environment so children can escape the noisier areas of the room during the day. Standardized classroom equipment in catalogs often does not meet the needs of young children in care for long periods of time. Also most budgets are geared to the purchase of paper and pencil items with "left over" dollars allocated for the purchase of "classroom equipment."

Today there are fewer, "leftover" dollars for equipment; this is a problem and creative teachers are designing equipment to be built by carpenters, competent parents and staff.

The classroom equipment in this text was designed for use in the Matthew R. Lowry Early Childhood Center at Oakland University and tested by many active children, undergraduate and graduate students, parents, faculty and staff.

Mastering physical feats on classroom equipment encourages success and the development of a strong self concept. Success, or the "achievement of something attempted" is attained by children when the physical environment supports success. The equipment discussed in this text provides a base for the success of young children in not only motor, but social and emotional development as well. Also thinking, problem solving and creativity is enhanced. Being successful is to achieve "a favorable outcome." (Morris, 1970)

Designing Effective Early Childhood Environments

To achieve this outcome, the equipment <u>must be challenging yet children</u> need to master it. Some equipment calls for individual exploration, while other dictates more social interaction, supporting goals and objectives in the curriculum and giving the room variety and character.

In Chapter V, there are illustrations of structures appropriate for early childhood classrooms. All are fairly simple in construction, inexpensive to implement, and can be modified for individual program needs and space. The drawings may stimulate ideas for other items or new curriculum. Curriculum is not a main focus in this text, however, suggestions are included with each piece of equipment to further exploration, expansion and involvement by the children. The equipment is organized from the least difficult to construct to the most difficult.

Classroom arrangements are illustrated to include the equipment into the classroom. Some diagrams show just a corner of a room while others illustrate two or three areas that are combined. Individual areas, such as library, art, block, manipulative, housekeeping, and science and mathematics, are described with suggestions for physical set up, as well as what materials could be included. Some dimensions (Noisy/Quiet, Simple/Complex, etc.) of the classroom are discussed to aid in arranging the room and making it more "homey" or inviting.

As children spend longer periods of time during the day in school, all programs must have flexible, inviting environments. No longer can we educate children in quiet environments filled with rows of desks and teachers who lecture in front of the classroom. We must meet the developmental needs of children and provide exciting learning experiences that encourage decision making, problem solving and creative thinking. The environments must enable children to move around, talk freely, and learn in a play-based environment. Only when these environments are the standard in every early childhood program and classroom, will we be educating children for the next century.

# CHAPTER I

# PHYSICAL ENVIRONMENT AFFECTS LEARNING

## Chapter Outline

- **Physical Environment Affects Learning**
- **A Learning Environment**
- **Importance of the Child**
- **Children Learn Through Action**
- **Importance of Movement**
- **Relating to Others**
- **Importance of Play**
- **Role of the Teacher**
- **Primary Classrooms**
- **Teaching Cooperation**
- **Questions on Chapter I**

Photo copyright April S. Haase

# CHAPTER I

# PHYSICAL ENVIRONMENT AFFECTS LEARNING

**Physical Environment Affects Learning**

The early childhood environment sets a stage where children can be explorers in a world they only slightly understand. As explorers, they will experience firsthand that sliding down a snow covered hill is easier than climbing back up; it takes strength and persistence to pull a loaded wagon; and cement is hard when they fall on it. All experiences help children understand the forces in the world and their relationship to and control of their environment. There is an element of stability in the physical environment that children can come to depend on and respect. (Blatz and Bott, 1930)

The physical environment has an important influence upon children and how they act upon it. (Mason, 1982) Of course, the biological/chemical, or genetic make up influences what human beings become, but the physical environment can be designed "to facilitate the development of human potential." (Zifferblatt, 1972) The physical environment is arranged to encourage desired behavior, small and large group activities, individual and teacher-assisted exploration, and easily accessible, overlapping work areas.

**A Learning Environment**

Children experience their surroundings by using what is available to them, including their senses, muscles, people, and (today) the electronic media. Electronic media does help children experience the ideas of their time. "Sight and sounds, tactile and visual experiences, kinesthetic and taste experiences and, of course, people, provide children concrete experiences for assimilating and accommodating the messages received by such experiences." (Robison, 1977)

Robison's definition of assimilation and accommodation to explain the developmental process of gathering concepts for cognitive development is:

> Assimilation is the process by which the child gives personal meanings and formulations to experiences and information. But this process can stray pretty far from reality. Accommodation is the checking process, permitting reality

to intrude and test the child's ideas and to press for elimination of gross distortions. The balancing process is continuous, with constant swings from reality to imagination. (p.34)

Movement or action in the environment gives each child the raw materials to assimilate and accommodate experiences and ideas to develop schemata. Development does not necessarily occur with action or movement alone, but is an interacting element with assimilation and accommodation to further cognitive development. (Wadsworth, 1971)

Whitehurst (1984) indicates movement means many things to the child. It is a way to discover self and the environment, both physically and socially. Movement means freedom to explore space and freedom for self-expression. Children's movement can show enjoyment, pleasure and acceptance by others. Movement helps them develop concepts about life.

**Importance of the Child**

Teachers, educators and parents seem to agree that early childhood programs should be a major force in the development of each child, for child is a total being, and the "physical, social, emotional and intellectual aspects of development depend on and support each other. These aspects are not separate and one should not be pushed ahead of the others." (A Gift of Time, 1982) Since these aspects depend on each other, the development of the whole child occurs when the child is active physically, mentally and emotionally. (Werner and Burton, 1979)

Both in and out of educational settings, children learn by doing. They are active participants in the world around them. As infants, their early responses are primarily motor--the basis for higher learning later in life. Children continue to respond to their world by handling objects, meeting new challenges, and even testing the rule of gravity, all using their bodies to explore the messages of these experiences. (Lerch et al., 1974)

**Children Learn Through Action**

The everyday environment should and does present endless opportunity for social interaction, creative expression, development of physical/motor skills, cooperation, feeling and thinking, as well as speaking and listening. In other words, the everyday environment should and does present endless opportunity for learning. (Fleming, 1968; Headley and Liddle, 1974)

"Learning or intelligence permeates all human activity and . . . (intelligence) is inseparably interrelated with emotions, social interaction, and physical activity. For children to become fully functioning human beings, there is a need to have contact with the real world and use all their senses, not just their visual and auditory sense." (Werner and Burton, 1979) With physical activity, children receive messages from all their senses--tactile (touching), kinesthetic (feeling), visual (seeing), auditory (hearing), olfactory (smelling), and gustatory (tasting)--which develop and sharpen their perceptions of the world. (Frost and Klein, 1983)

Actions, instead of long discussions, are what young children need to experience in order to learn. Obviously, children enter into more complex discussions as language develops and experiences expand, but for young children, a developing cognition is based on "doing".

"This physical action of movement with objects or space forces children to receive and process information so they know the look, the feel, and the sense of what is happening. Children are participants in the world around them because they are surrounded, enfolded, and engulfed by the environment and they cannot be isolated from it." (Canter, 1977)

The child uses accumulated experiences from interactions with the environment to make comparisons to previous schemata of "pictures" stored in the mind. Schemata of the child's world are constantly in a state of change; refined through new information in the assimilation and accommodation process. This expands the child's cognitive development and understanding of reality.

**Importance of Movement**

Movement in a classroom, whether through music or on climbers, allows children to express creativity, high spirits and the joy of developing their bodies in challenging new ways. A child's movements influences psychological abilities. How the self concept of the child develops is influenced to a large extent by accomplishing motor acts in an environment that supports action and autonomy, or independence, of the young child. (Omwake, 1984)

For example, experiences such as rolling a ball, climbing through a tire, reaching the top of the slide and sliding down are all accomplishments and achievements in which children feel successful. Movement, such as smashing a sand castle, throwing a ball against a wall, or singing at the top of the lungs, can all be a release of pressure, anxiety and anger. (Frostig, 1970)

Achievements and release of tensions contribute to a healthy personality, as do physical activity, creative movement and excitement. "Children need active experiences to use their growing muscles and to strengthen their growing concepts." (Robison, 1977) The activity is their participation with the environment at hand. This interaction with the environment also gives the child a sense of belonging. (Blake, 1968) The child asks the question: "Can this place be mine?" And the answer should be a positive one. Using art materials in new ways or building new structures with blocks shows a creative individual. These experiences also answer the question, "Can I produce results?" The "what if" question also is explored when new risks are taken.

**Relating to Others**

During physical or movement activities, the child answers the question, how can I relate to others? Movement helps children to communicate and understand the approval of others. Grabbing another child's toy sends one message (or more), whereas helping someone walk the balance beam is quite a different message. Whether the child grabs a toy or helps with the balancing act, more than likely, there is response from the other individual, forcing the first child to make a judgement or perception of the situation. This judgement will prod the child to continue, stop and leave, exert more control, or to compromise. (Proshansky and Wolfe, 1975)

The interaction of the child with the environment can be intense. Children are always learning from the environment. It is motivating and exciting to children when it is possible to choose what they want to learn. However, children also need space and time to play. (Federlein, 1989; Robison, 1977; Taylor and Vlastos, 1975) There is a need for physical space, as well as emotional space. Children need uninterrupted long periods of time to explore, experience and manipulate materials in the learning environment. Good early childhood programs for infants, toddlers, preschoolers and children in kindergarten through third grade, provide ample time and space on a daily basis.

**Importance of Play**

The physical environment helps foster the learning process in young children, but it is early childhood trained teachers who understand the importance of play in the learning process, movement and how to construct a successful learning environment. No one definition is sufficient to describe the term play. Some definitions include words such as spontaneous, recreation or personal satisfaction. Play also is described as a child's business or work, or how the child experiences the world to develop new concepts. (Frost and Klein, 1983)

Creative exploration, experimenting, constructing, combining, and manipulating objects in the environment also characterize play. Many educators and philosophers have commented on the importance of play. Karl Gross developed his theory of surplus energy with regard to play. The theory defines play as the need to get rid of excess energy. Greek philosophers Plato and Aristotle recognized the healthy development in children when they played and its necessity in the education of young children. Rousseau and Froebel refuted the benefits of rote learning, in favor of play as the medium for learning. The Cognitive Development Theory by Jean Piaget states play is both a "vehicle for knowing about the world and a product or indicator of the child's level of cognitive development." (Frost and Klein, 1983) John Dewey, the modern day educational philosopher, supports play and defines it, "As the child plays he builds up a storehouse of concepts and a world of meanings, all of which are essential to intellectual growth." (Butler, 1978)

Early childhood educators contend that play is purposeful and the individual child at play is a whole person engaging in taking from the environment what is needed and desired; internalizing these elements; and changing the self and perception of the world in the process. (Shipley and Carpenter, 1962)

The physical environment takes into account the child's need to interact. Learning, or cognitive growth, occurs through physical and active involvement with the environment. Early childhood educators support physical activity of children and often say "children learn through talking and doing, that is, through messing around in a planned environment with appropriate materials and equipment." (Federlein, 1989) Active learning is supported in the philosophy of the British Infant School. "Active doing is the best way to learn." (Taylor and Vlastos, 1975) Leela C. Zion and Betty Lou Raker state, "Mental processing is the result of a functioning body." Piaget purports that perceptual activities influence cognitive behavior throughout the learning process and all concepts must be taught through activity. (Wadsworth, 1971)

> Learning depends upon the structure of and the child's interaction with the environment. "All children come to schools with needs. It is the responsibility of the school to do its best to meet these needs." (Mante and Mathisen, 1977)

**Role of the Teacher**

Although the arrangement of furniture and the building of specific equipment for early childhood classrooms are focuses, the role of the early childhood teacher in setting up the environment is crucial. Teachers need to assess 1-developmental characteristics of children, 2- how to effectively integrate these needs into:

- space of the classroom
- number of children
- storage available
- category of equipment and materials
- amount of equipment and materials
- new traffic patterns.

The environment needs to address the needs for representational play of the younger children and more symbolic play of older children. At first, toddlers need objects to represent their world on a concrete level. Symbolic play develops in preschoolers and early primary age children who do not need as much support from objects and teacher involvement.

Primary age children miniaturize their play in the classroom and learn through playing games. Teachers can design the classroom to include equipment for specific uses, as well as materials for imaginative use. For example, if a teacher creates the neighborhood as a play activity, the young child needs many props, such as blocks and boxes to build a hospital, post office, garage, grocery store, mall and gas stations.

Older children have had more experiences with creating structures so they use a variation of blocks or other materials in the classroom to build an entire city. The children then expand the building into dramatic play with each child taking a role as a different "worker" after the construction is completed. All too often in primary classrooms there are no materials or equipment to encourage learning through play. For many elementary teachers, play is only for preschool programs. Teachers must be trained to understand and appreciate children's abilities and development. Although it is important that teachers assist children to improve skills and gain new knowledge, an early childhood trained teacher also encourages a child to accept strengths within oneself, including mastery of specific skills.

For example, children with cerebral palsy may learn to walk and talk by three years of age, but need to understand the physical limitations of cerebral palsy, how to accept it and when to ask for help. Children who react emotionally to most situations may need help in channeling their outbursts in more socially accepted ways. Teachers assist young children in accepting and helping each other to use acceptable behavior; thus socialization occurs much earlier in children who have participated in groups. (Lay-Dopera, Dopera, 1990)

Early childhood teachers must know developmental characteristics and the wide range of "normal" behavior to provide appropriate learning experiences. Different activity areas in the early childhood classroom provide for action, conversation, social play and privacy. Exercise for growing muscles and coordination of the body is provided when climbing structures, large blocks and open areas are used for running and throwing. Whereby conversation or language development is continually encouraged throughout all areas of the curriculum and in every activity.

**Primary Classrooms**

In primary grade classrooms the same kinds of provisions must be made. Children in kindergarten through third grade continue to need freedom to move about, investigate, experiment, curl up with a good book, or find a nook away from everyone else. It is up to the teacher to provide opportunities for creative movement, song, dance, as well as coordination practice with ball skills, tumbling and the ever popular emergent team sport participation.

Social play and interaction must permeate all areas, but children sometimes "seek a place to work and play away from teachers, and sometimes even away from fellow classmates. Schools which simply provide open physical space do not provide for this need." (Taylor and Vlastos, 1975) Individual drawing areas, raised platforms with crawl spaces underneath and mirrors for self-awareness all provide personal space and quiet time for children who spend long hours in the classroom.

Social interaction is generally discouraged in the primary grades and teachers are trained to conduct quiet, orderly classrooms. But, times are changing. No longer is individual accomplishment valued in the work place. In their adult lives, children will likely work on teams to solve problems or produce a product. Cooperative group learning and sharing ideas with each other are crucial for optimal learning now, and to begin to prepare children for their contribution to society in the future. (Johnson and Johnson, 1983)

The physical arrangement of each area affects the number of participants and type of participation by each child. For example, painting can be done alone at a single easel or with others when easels are placed side by side on a wall. A raised platform in a corner of the classroom is inviting and gives a different view. Water and sand tables encourage both individual exploration and sharing.

Remember, very young children do not understand sharing, so plenty of funnels and measuring cups should be provided. If an item becomes a "favorite," add many more to eliminate unnecessary conflict. Older children are less egocentric, so fewer objects can be placed in the table to encourage sharing and teamwork. These activity centers encouraging development in physical, social-emotional, cognitive and language areas are appropriate in all early childhood classrooms, including primary grades.

**Teaching Cooperation**

Teaching cooperation and sharing are concerns of teachers, and the physical environment, if designed for young children, encourages both. The arrangement of the room should be orderly and uncluttered so children know where materials are kept. Staff must model teamwork, cooperation and respect for one another. If cooperation, rather than competition, is stressed, children will model what they see, learning to respect and develop sharing characteristics.

Classroom materials used regularly should be accessible to children to encourage independence and autonomy. However, there are many materials only the teacher uses and the selection depends on the developmental age of the child. With younger children, only markers and paper are out on the art table at the beginning of the year. However, as the year progresses, items are added to or exchanged, depending on the skills to be learned. The skills and social abilities of the group needs to be assessed to encourage sharing and optimum use of materials. This principle is applicable to primary grade children as well. Too many choices confuse the child. However, if a particular item is requested, teachers should acknowledge the child's initiative and supply the material.

The same materials are used differently by children in different developmental stages. For instance, toddlers use blocks to mouth and then eventually build towers with one or two blocks. Cylinder blocks are used as drinking glasses. Preschool children may use a few blocks to build a house or garage for their cars. Later, in first and second grades, these same children construct three dimensional enclosed structures with roads, spaceships or castles to expand on their dramatic play. Adults, such as architects, use blocks to construct complex structures on the job.

Teachers are the critical factor creating an exciting, effective learning environment; one with appropriate activities and equipment for the unconditional nurturing of children. The teacher designs an early childhood environment that allows children to develop autonomy, problem solving, and decision making skills in an accepting environment that is supportive of diversity and creativity.

**Large and Small Groups**

Sometimes all children do an activity at the same time, and at other times individually, (especially if the aim is to nurture specific skills). There also are small groups of children learning through play. If a large group activity is scheduled, materials are brought to a centralized work area. However, if individual or small group learning is expected, then more activity centers are set up around the classroom for individuals or small groups of children. A balance between individual, small, and large group experiences are necessary for optimum development of all children. The learning environment is always flexible enough to provide appropriate challenges for all children, based on the developmental levels in all four areas: social/emotional, cognitive, physical and languages. Often the range of development in each area is three to four years. No longer does the standardized curriculum meet the needs of young children.

Guidelines to support individualized learning, as well as encourage children to initiate activities and learn respect for self and others will be discussed in later chapters. Most early childhood classrooms already provide some guidelines, but few have an ongoing evaluation process to assess the learning in each child. Suggestions for evaluation methods also will be discussed.

## Questions for Chapter I

1. Identify ways to discuss with parents how children learn through play.

2. Outline a justification for learning through play to administrators.

3. Develop a presentation for the community on play based environments

4. Compare how you are being educated in teacher education programs to the role you will assume as a teacher in an early childhood classroom.

5. What new early childhood components should be added to the teacher education program at your institution?

Photo copyright April S. Haase

# Chapter II

# Promoting Movement in Early Childhood Environments

## Chapter Outline

- Movement is Necessary
- Development of Language
- Social Skills Cognition
- Associations Learned
- Blocks, Blocks, Blocks
- Questions for Chapter II

Designing Effective Early Childhood Environments

Photo copyright April S. Haase

# CHAPTER II

# PROMOTING MOVEMENT IN EARLY CHILDHOOD ENVIRONMENTS

**Movement is Necessary**

Everyone moves for one reason or another, such as for safety, relaxation, getting somewhere or satisfying inner motivations. People run up and give a hug to an old friend, or walk for exercise and sight-seeing. They become tense and avoid eye contact when corrected for too much inappropriate movement. And when movement is hindered, adults, as well as children, become passive, negative, explosive, or defensive. (Shipley and Carpenter, 1962)

Movement enhances the ability to focus one's attention and to exert control. Time and space dimensions and awareness of the physical environment are sharpened through movement. (Frostig, 1970) Children need challenges. They need to try different activities and ways of relating to others. Equipment that allows for movement meets these challenges. (Robison, 1977)

Goals in effective early childhood programs address all areas of development: physical, language, social/emotional and cognitive. Specifically, physical activity is necessary for learning in young children because:

1- they learn holistically and use their whole being when actively involved in learning,

2- they learn through doing, not through extensive discussions,

3- the results or outcomes are immediate and observable.

Physical activity helps children to understand balance and to identify reference points within their bodies. Knowing one's own body parts and how they work independently and together, and knowing one's position in space establishes the child's "body image." If the body image is not established, the child overestimates how much space is needed to engage in movement and activities. (Kephart, 1975) Body awareness also helps a child understand the separateness and independence from others, the environment and world. (Frostig, 1970)

## Development of Language, Social Skills and Cognition

Language also is enhanced through movement and manipulation of objects. Objects are labeled by others around the child. Through shared dialogue, a true understanding of up, down, light, heavy, over, under, top and bottom develops. Understanding of words and symbols becomes stronger through literally moving the body to learn the relationship of a word or symbol to the action. Movement is a means of expression and supplements words. (Werner and Burton, 1979) Feelings of satisfaction can be achieved when a new skill, such as skipping, is learned. Feelings of adequacy and belonging occur when a child pushes a peer on the swing. Children who do not have strong language skills (and even those who do) can use movement to help others understand their message.

Social adjustment occurs through movement. (Frostig, 1970) Knowing how to move through space and how much power and control a child has of the body enhances social relationships. Taking turns, for example, shows the child is learning respect for others. Helping another child carry some toys or finish a puzzle teaches cooperation and develops leadership abilities. Sharing materials and work during project construction reinforces these concepts.

A great number of cognitive skills are learned through movement. Exploring materials firsthand gives children a chance to perceive objects in their true form. They can come to identify shapes and colors by playing with toys, furniture and other materials. Children understand nearby, larger than, smaller than, circular and round. (Holloway, 1967) Classification occurs when arranging same-size blocks on shelves, hanging pots and pans on pegboards or matching buckets filled with toys to the shelf where the picture of the toy is displayed. (Mante and Mathisen, 1977)

These activities assist children to place symbols and pictures on a page making it readable. It helps young children to be able to "read" a book and anticipate when it is time to turn the page. Children learn mathematical concepts through movement. If there is a limit of four children at one time allowed on a certain climber and three children are on it, how many more can play? Also, one-to-one correspondence is reinforced when pegs are put in holes; when one cup per child is needed at snack; and when one hat to one hook is matched. The language of mathematics is learned when primary age children build patterns with attributes of themselves, as they could while snapping and clapping to act out various patterns.

Structuring lessons to teach science is easy for teachers when they realize science is not taught, but rather investigated. Science is everywhere. Children learn about forces and gravity when jumping off raised areas, throwing a ball, pulling or pushing a wagon, or pouring juice. They learn about the sun, ground, seeds, lightness and darkness when taking care of plants. They experience the seasons. They see their ice cream melt. They learn about the effects of erosion when water comes out the downspout. They watch potatoes get mashed, boiled and baked. They learn time by the repetition of actions or days. (Robison, 1977)

Young children learn about time when they realize what comes "before" or "after." They learn predictability of future actions when they learn to wait their turn to go down the slide. (Frostig, 1970) They understand space because they move in it. They learn to think in a step-by-step scientific manner during play and when a teacher models for them. In too many primary classrooms, active learning diminishes as the child gets older and is replaced by rote learning through ditto sheets and workbooks. In spite of this practice, primary children need to learn by doing to establish a firm base for future learning.

**Associations Learned**
Many associations can be learned through movement as identified by Marianne Frostig and Phyllis Maslow (1970). They are:

Visual-motor association. Examples are using eyes and hands when catching a ball, guiding a magnet along a marked trail, or holding one magnet on top of a surface and another underneath to guide the first one.

Visual-motor transfer. This is reproducing a movement, such as turning around once in place, after watching someone else demonstrate it.

Auditory-motor association is exemplified by dancing to music or interpreting pitch or tones with heavy steps in accordance with low sounds and light steps for high sounds.

Auditory-motor transfer reproduces a sequence, such as clapping pattern to beat or hand jive sequence.

Motor-kinesthetic association involves balancing one's body walking or crossing a balance beam. Body awareness exercises are included in early childhood programs so a child identifies the body parts in song or in mirror reflections.

Tactile-motor association occurs when children use their senses with movement in activities, such as tracing sandpaper letters while blindfolded.

## Blocks, Blocks, Blocks

Teachers and parents often ask if the child is learning while moving around. A good example is when a child uses blocks. The basic unit blocks, developed by Caroline Pratt, an American educator, are one of the most important materials in early childhood curricula. A set is based on a proportion of 1:2:4. They are half as high as they are wide, and twice as long as they are wide. (Provenzo and Brett, 1983) Blocks enhance learning in reading, language, math, science, sociodramatic play, emotional growth and perceptual motor areas.

Children's reading skills can improve "through the patterning and shaping experience blocks provide and in the planning and sequencing of the building construction." (Robison, 1977) The naming of the blocks and structures increases vocabulary and social language is increased when more than one child is involved in the construction.

Number concepts are learned through blocks, such as one to one correspondence, counting, sets, categorization, area, squares, measurement and patterning. The basics of science are internalized through block building because they are three-dimensional. Therefore, properties of matter, thickness, width and length are learned. Children learn positional relationships when placing blocks flat, on edge or on end. (Hirsch, 1974) The pull of gravity is experienced when balancing blocks and trying to stabilize a structure and finally children learn that structure consists of parts that make a whole.

Blocks extend sociodramatic play and language is practiced when children tell stories about the structures or expand the play scenarios. Fantasies and fears are played out with this medium and field trips are re-created. Information gathered from books, films and discussions is reconstructed and embellished by children through block building.

Pride is evident when a tower or structure is complete and the child experiences accomplishment. Blocks provide a challenge children can meet and thus achieve success. Blocks also provide an outlet for aggression through banging and crashing constructions. (Robison, 1977)

Blocks help children learn about vertical and horizontal space and the differences between the two. They learn properties of enclosed space, how to duplicate architectural patterns, grid patterns, and directionality; all important skills contributing to the future development of more complex functions.

Balance is learned through building towers, walls or bridges. A "feel" for gravity is observed when towers fall or cars roll down a ramp. Enclosure is learned when a bridge, tunnel or fort is constructed. Depth perception is experienced when the child discovers the front and back of an object and the distance between the blocks, thereby understanding the properties of three dimensional objects.

The concept of "lateral" is understood in learning the various sides of blocks are different, i.e., edge, flat, end. Directionality is an extension of the awareness of laterality. Lining up blocks horizontally and building at various angles demonstrates an understanding of directionality.

Dynamic balance is enhanced when building with blocks because the child uses the body to maintain equilibrium while creating with blocks. Hand-eye coordination is developed through block building, as are fine and gross motor skills. Small blocks help small muscles develop control, particularly the eyes and hands. Larger muscles are developed through the use of unit or large hollow blocks. There is development of figure ground when children look for a certain block among the shelves of many different shapes and colors of blocks. Figure ground is important in the reading process because it is the ability to see letters and words separate from the page.

Spatial awareness and position in space are both strongly developed through playing with blocks. Whether blocks are used vertically, horizontally or in architectural patterns, they take up and define space. Spatial relationships in a block structure include up, down, right, left, over, under, above, below, before, behind, on top, backward, forward, tiny, huge, far, near, similar and different. Children through the primary grades can profit from experiences with blocks. All first, second and third grade classrooms should contain many sets of blocks both large and small.

Blocks are important in the development of concepts in the young child, as are all materials and equipment that encourage action and movement.

## Questions for Chapter II

1. Create a unit on movement to teach in an early childhood program.

2. How are the language, social/emotional and cognitive areas developed in movement?

3. What are the developmental stages children go through when building with blocks?

4. Justify the use of blocks in primary grades.

5. Debate whether young children should be in formalized movement programs.

# CHAPTER III

# DESIGNING EARLY CHILDHOOD CLASSROOMS

**Chapter Outline**

- Environment Has Two Elements
- Basic Requirements
- Size of the Classroom
- Number of Children
- Storage Units
- Evaluation of Equipment and Materials
- Structuring Paths Between Centers
- Dimensions to Include in Designing a Classroom
- Designing Curricular Centers
- Summary
- Evaluate the Environment
- Questions for Chapter III

Designing Effective Early Childhood Environments

Photo copyright April S. Haase

# CHAPTER III

# DESIGNING EARLY CHILDHOOD CLASSROOMS

## Environment Has Two Elements

The early childhood physical environment consists of two elements: architectural structure and arranged environment. They form the ecology that supports learning.

The architectural structure provides and establishes space, light, sound, temperature, color, texture, levels, curves, angles, access to the outside, and fixed or movable structures.

The arranged environment requires organizing spaces and material to support physical actions of learners as they go about their work. (Loughlin and Suina, 1982) The following suggestions expand on the practical aspects of these two elements.

## Basic Requirements

* Early childhood classrooms must meet fire and safety requirements with clearly marked exits, outlet covers and fire extinguishers. There should be at least two exits from the building.

* Bathroom facilities in good working condition, sized and installed to fit young children should be adjacent or within the classroom.

* A minimum of 35 square feet per child in the classroom is mandated by most states. Early childhood professionals suggest up to 100 feet per child with the outdoor area between 50 to 200 square feet per child.

* Equipment must be in excellent condition; free of protrusions, rough surfaces and broken parts.

* Climbing equipment must always be placed over soft surfaces to avoid injury.

* Floor space should be free of drafts and cleaned daily.

Designing Effective Early Childhood Environments

* Adequate lighting is a must.

* Carpeting should cover areas where children play on the floor. Carpeting the walls subdues noise. Tiled areas are preferred for water and painting activities. If the room is carpeted, a piece of heavy vinyl can be taped to the carpet and be swept or mopped like a tile floor. The vinyl sheeting should have a rough surface so it will not be slippery when wet.

## Size of the Classroom

Space determines movement and physical behaviors of a group. Whether designing a new classroom or rearranging an existing environment, begin by drawing the room to scale on graph paper.

* Include all permanent equipment such as sinks, outlets, lights, blackboards, storage cabinets, windows and doors.

* Draw several arrangements to 'play around' in the best environment.

* Divide the room into four areas based on activities in the area: noisy, quiet, wet and dry. Consider the permanent fixtures when dividing the room.

* Place the art area near a water source.

* Separate noisy areas from quiet ones. If more than one room is available, separate the activities, and if all the children stay in one room, design the noisy and quiet areas carefully.

* Arrange the room so the teacher can see all areas.

* Make materials accessible to the children on low shelving units.

* Minimize the number of tables and chairs in the room. Every child does not need a chair. Remember Table + Chair + Child = 10 Legs! In primary rooms, desks should be selected for their versatility of arrangement.

* Determine where large group activities will be held and how frequently the equipment must be moved.

## Number of Children

* The number of activities going on concurrently is in direct proportion to the number of children. Each center needs multiple activities developing a wide range of skills.

Chapter 3: Designing Effective Childhood Environment

* Allow ample space for privacy, as well as snacks and lunch.

* Arrange 'on the floor' space for children to be near props and materials to expand their learning and skills.

* Design an area with a specific number of children in mind.

* Provide activities for at least one and one-half times the number of children in the room. For example, if ten children are playing in a room, a minimum of 15 activities are provided. Having more activities than the number of children allows children to make choices about their learning and not waste time 'waiting' for a turn. Multiple choices encourage flexibility in the classroom and the development of decision making skills, problem solving abilities, and creative thinking; all contributing in the development of a healthy self concept and sense of autonomy.

* In a primary classroom a minimum of twelve centers is suggested. The are library, art, a unit of integrated learning, easel, mathematics, sensory, writing--including a computer, fine motor, science, cooking, pets, blocks, music and listening.

**Storage Units**

* Keep storage of the teacher's materials to a minimum inside the classroom. A large central storage area away from the classroom is more efficient. An example of a teacher's storage unit and child's space can be found in the appendices.

* A variety of classroom materials must be accessible to children.

* Mark all storage areas so equipment and materials can be easily returned by both children and adults.

* Use open shelving for storage. Doors interfere with interest, space and replacing equipment. Shelves should not be cluttered. Materials should be stored side-by-side, rather than stacked for easy viewing. Materials should be changed from time to time for variety. When they are not being used by children, they should be stored in a dry, closed cupboard, preferably in an adjacent area.

* Keep storage units in the area where children use the materials for easy access.

## Designing Effective Early Childhood Environments

**Evaluation of Equipment and Materials**

The amount of equipment and materials is determined to some extent by the number of children, room size and funds available. Making a list of what materials are available and their use determines what kind of space is needed -- large, open spaces or soft, cozy alcoves.

Equipment is evaluated by its contribution to the goals of the program. (Butler et al., 1978) Use these suggestions when selecting equipment for new or established programs.

**Equipment**

1. Practically speaking, the most important criteria for selecting early childhood equipment and materials is cost. Cost must be weighed against benefits. Is a more expensive item that is long lasting better than a cheaper, less durable item? A room does not need to contain the most expensive equipment. Getting full use of what is in the room is the important criteria. To cut down on costs, parents, teachers, and community volunteers can help build equipment or donate items needed. Remember to obtain legal advice on the liability of the program if equipment is constructed by volunteers.

2. Check the quality and durability of all equipment, as well as what kind of upkeep is needed.

3. Examine safety equipment. There must be no protrusions, finishes on the equipment must be non-toxic and large equipment must safely hold the weight of more than one or two children.

4. Furniture needs to be child-sized.

5. Assess the size of equipment. If it is large and encourages large muscle play, plenty of room will be needed around the structure for running, walking and crawling.

6. Check for flexibility. Can the equipment be used in a variety of ways? Is it necessary for the development of certain skills? Determine if a structure is flexible or if there are only one or two uses for the piece of equipment.

7. Wherever possible, label the furniture or storage unit areas with pictures and words. Children will learn where materials belong and become aware of the relationship between pictures and words or "reading." This is useful at the beginning of the year in first grade, as well.

Chapter 3: Designing Effective Childhood Environment

## Materials

1. When selecting materials consider the chronological and developmental ages of children, interests, physical size, any physical impediments, safety and program goals. The ages, interests, and learning abilities of the group should be matched to all materials. This is as true in the primary grades as it is in preschool and kindergarten.

2. When displaying materials on a shelf, ask the following questions: does the material have all the parts? Are there separate attractive containers for various materials? Are there enough materials for the group? Are the shelves crowded? Can the children return the materials easily?

## Structuring Paths Between Centers

* The child's environment is different than that of the adult because of the child's size. Teachers should position themselves in the spaces where children work and move to define a path. Reach the child's level by kneeling or stooping. Check for any interference along paths near play activities.

* Paths are broad, elongated and separate differing play areas. However, if they are too wide or long, children run back and forth. Teachers then must make necessary adjustments, such as placing furniture at angles.

* Limit the entrances so children know where they are going. Children need to learn how to get through a space. A broad enough path will ensure less congestion and a quick route to an activity.

* Avoid having activities in a pathway or any changes of level in the route. Pathways should go around an area, not through.

* Remember, the same principles apply in primary classrooms.

## Dimensions to Include in Designing a Classroom

* **Softness/Hardness.** Soft areas have certain limits and provide tactile experiences that hard surfaces do not. Soft areas will allow children to use materials in different ways, and encourage leisure and relaxation.

* **Open/Closed.** Plenty of open ended materials, such as collage materials, sand, blocks and dress up materials should be provided. Blocks, collage materials and a painting easel should be included for primary grade children, as well. Closed materials, such as puzzles, books and lotto games, also are

needed in both settings.

* **Simple/Complex.** A simple material, such as sand, can be made more complex by adding digging equipment to encourage problem solving, decision making and creative thinking. Older children will use these materials in more complex ways suitable to their age group.

* **Intrusions/Seclusion.** Some areas will allow occupancy by many children at one time. The space also must include areas for privacy for one or two children at a time.

* **High Mobility/Low Mobility.** Activities and equipment are provided for both large muscle and small muscle movement. Primary grade children also need this opportunity to move about and develop muscle coordination.

* **Noisy/Quiet.** Areas in the room are placed so that the noisier areas are to one side or corner and the quieter areas are on the opposite side. This eliminates teachers quieting down children so others can hear. Children in the primary grades should be permitted to converse while using centers.

* **Wet/Dry.** These two dimensions also work with noisy/quiet. They can be combined to divide a room into four areas: noisy/wet, noisy/dry, quiet/wet and quiet/dry. The noisy/wet areas contain the water table, clay, cooking, and/or art activity. The noisy/dry area contains a wide range of blocks, manipulatives, puzzles, clay, woodworking or dress up clothes. The quiet/wet area houses the science center, collage area, easels or painting activities. The quiet/dry area has the books, writing area, puzzles, math and drawing areas.

* **Neatness/Cluttered.** If areas are cluttered, it is difficult for children to find desirable materials and they quickly lose interest. However, during all activities "messiness" and noise are expected for young children. They are expected to clean up after the activity and leave the area just as neat as they found it.

Work towards a balance of all these dimensions in the classroom, as they allow children to manipulate and experience a variety of learning activities. Youngsters are encouraged to socialize, be alone or be creative within built-in limits. The structure, design and activities in the classroom provide the necessary limits for all children. This is called the "velvet hammer". Children are aware of limits in the environment or during the activity, but are not constantly reminded by the adults. When these implicit controls are used, children develop internal controls for behavior, rather than rely on authority to define the limits. Allowing the children to be in control of their own learning and to make choices is part of a quality early childhood program. Children in infant programs through third grade can profit from this environment.

## Designing Curricular Centers

There are seven activity areas in early childhood classrooms that individualize a program and frees the teacher from constantly interrupting children and dispensing materials. Define each area with signs over the activity center and identify the learning taking place. This eliminate unnecessary interference from adults in the classroom asking what the children are learning and what they are 'doing'. The seven areas are:

### Art Area

* The art area should be near a sink if possible, but a bucket of warm, soapy water can be placed nearby for initial rinsing of hands before leaving to go to the sink.

* Tables provide good flat working surfaces. Have one table off to the side for up to four primary aged (five to nine year old) children to draw. A larger table for three years olds is needed because they are the "we" group and need space for six to eight at one time. Four, five and six year olds like to draw in pairs. Therefore, both areas are needed if there are multiple age groups in the class. Both areas also need the same supplies so children are not travelling around the room to get supplies, losing direction and finding other activities.

* Easels are beneficial. They provide individual space or when two are placed on a wall together, there is social development. Provide marking pens as well so children can record ideas on their paintings. Easels should be in all preschool and primary classrooms.

* Match the floor and tables to the activity. Surfaces must be easy to clean. If the floor is carpeted, tape a shower curtain or piece of vinyl to the floor for easy clean up. Be sure the surface is textured so it will not be slippery when wet. Thick, clear plastic can be taped to table tops that are hard to clean. Plastic or newspaper help protect table tops.

* Make paper, glue, tape, scissors, markers, crayons, stamps and ink pads, chalk, pencils, pens and hole punchers accessible. Consider the ages of the children for optimum use of materials, and rotate them for variety.

* Have smocks available for messy activities and designate a place for storage.

* A drying area should be nearby with flat surfaces for "drippy" creations and clothes pins on lines for creations that can "hang dry." Most shelf areas provide flat surfaces for drying, or string can be hung by windows, between heating pipes (if exposed) or along the bottom of a chalkboard.

### Science Area

* Give optimum opportunities for children to explore items with magnifying glasses, feel different textures, compare, order, classify, measure, weigh, balance, and observe. A water source and electrical outlet should be close by.

### Dramatic Play Area

* Place all housekeeping equipment here for children to rearrange to extend creative play. Change equipment or "props" weekly or monthly, depending on the interest of the children. Encourage primary age children to bring materials from home to correlate with units of study.

* Lofts create "more" space by providing a first level and an "upstairs." The activities in each area can be totally different; upstairs can have pillows and books, while downstairs is a spaceship ready to take off for the moon. Lofts in primary grades increase space for activity centers.

* Put storage for dress up clothes near the loft or dramatic play area. Add hooks for increased storage and change accessories often. For example, a spaceship includes helmets, ear phones, walkie-talkies, steering wheels, computers, binoculars, telescopes and "moon" rocks to touch and explore with magnifying glasses. Social studies activities are included in this area. More suggestions are included with the loft design in the next chapter.

### Block or Construction Area

* Designate one-third of the total floor space for block building, with a dual purpose such as creative movement or lunch.

* If blocks are near the dramatic play area, learning through play is extended. Add different kinds of blocks, plastic people, plastic furniture, cars and planes to enhance creative thinking. Both areas need to be away from paths and doors. All primary grade classrooms also should have unit blocks, as well as props and small blocks, for greatly enhanced learning through block play.

* A variety of shapes, lengths and types of blocks is important, but an ample number of each kind is a necessity. Examine the blocks periodically for damage, splinters and cracking, removing, repairing and replacing on a regular basis.

* Use tape to delineate the boundaries of the block area. Taped designs within the space challenges children to use the blocks in innovative ways.

\* Add a tightly woven carpet in the block area to reduce some of the noise involved in construction. A low, carpeted platform could be used to facilitate construction on top, under, or around the platform. (See platform construction in Chapter V.)

\* Use long, low storage shelves for blocks and group them together. Bright colored construction paper shapes cut to the size of the blocks and affixed to the shelves with clear contact paper shows children where each type of block is stored. This also helps the child learn how to differentiate, sort and categorize while putting blocks away.

\* A woodworking table with real tools and vises should be available in primary classrooms. This area requires an adult nearby.

### Manipulative Area(s)

\* There are different areas in the room for manipulatives: one for math and /or science and others for small muscle activities.

\* Tables are best for math, science and puzzles, although puzzles also are used on the floor.

\* Math and science tables are designed for a small number of children to use at one time. Place them out of pathways and away from doors. The older child will enjoy these areas for exploration and practicing the concepts learned. Younger children prefer to manipulate materials in the wider environment. They develop conceptual understanding by practicing many skills at one time, such as matching one to one and sequencing. Mark storage areas clearly and place them next to the "work" area.

### Library Area

\* Plenty of books should be available. A card display unit from a local store can be cut in two. Use the top of the unit to display books, and replace library books weekly. Place books pertinent to units of study in a special place in the library for children.

\* The library 'nook' should be quiet, well lighted and comfortable. A slightly raised area with pillows or small rockers can give a sense of privacy. A table and chairs serves as a listening center, with writing tools and a story-on-a-tape recorder. (Construction of book platform see Chapter III.)

### Privacy Places

\* Sometimes these areas can be found where one would least expect...under a teacher's desk, behind a door, on a low shelf, under a table, in the doll bed, or in any corner. They allow children to escape noisier areas and encouragequiet activities. Children are able to rest, reflect and learn from watching others.

* Build privacy places into the classroom, such as quiet book areas. The top of a loft is a wonderful place to watch the "world." Teachers' storage units can also be built to have some "cubby" areas underneath for reading or flannel board play. (See Storage Cubby design in the next chapter.)

**Summary**

Consider all the guidelines and qualities of each activity area before beginning a new design. Not every room is easy to arrange or rearrange. Cluttered areas inhibit play and frustrate children and teachers have to "play" with the classroom design to achieve balance. Bare and open spaces are not inviting, so experiment with many designs and construct new spaces when rearranging an existing classroom.

For example, if the room has high ceilings, construct multi-level platforms for dramatic play areas below and privacy areas above. Add canopies and parachutes to lower the ceiling over different areas.

* Use different textures and/or colors on storage cabinets, such as flannel boards on the front or sides. Storage shelves on wheels can allow moving the materials to different areas and creating larger or smaller areas, depending upon the need. Create curves with structures or wall hangings to break up a room that is too rectangular. Remember tables used for puzzles or manipulatives are also used for lunch and snack.

* Add novelty to the room by moving the equipment. Put climbers with planks or ladders near a window, or place the ladder at a new angle or the climber on its side. Use blankets to create new spaces and creative thinking of "old" equipment. Alternate creative ways of using equipment with using it "correctly." This increases the value of each piece in the classroom.

Building different levels into the classroom gives variety, creates new spaces and cuts down on the authoritarian height of the teacher. If teachers do not frequently get down on the floor, the child is always looking up. The levels give the child a chance for more eye to eye contact. (Taylor and Vlastos, 1975) The raised platform design in the next chapter is not heavy and can be pulled out from the wall to create new spaces and possibilities for learning.

## Evaluation of the Environment

These suggestions are good only if the teacher spends time observing the children interacting with the environment and understands the needs of the children. The teacher's knowledge of child development and concern for a complete and well-rounded curriculum is enhanced by constructing an effective physical environment. Primary grade teachers need to spend more time observing children actively learning instead of always directly teaching.

The teacher's involvement with the children will give cues to improving the early childhood environment. Assess the classroom by collecting this data monthly. Another adult, such as a parent, volunteer or older student can assist. Develop a form to include:

1. Record of the children learning at each center.

2. Length of time spent in an area.

3. Proper use of an area or equipment and improper use of an area or equipment.

4. Rearrangement of equipment within an area.

5. Frequency of active versus passive activities.

Identify consistent problems in the classroom. Can they be remedied by changing traffic patterns, or use of materials? Take one problem at a time and diagnose the contributing factors. Then take time, rearrange and recreate learning areas one at a time until the problem is solved. Only work on one problem at a time to reduce further confusion for all children. Enlist the children's help. They will remind each other of agreed upon standards and rules.

## Questions for Chapter III

1. Design a floor plan for a preschool program. Identify the ages of the children, number enrolled and what pieces of equipment will be purchased or constructed on site.

2. Design a floor plan for a primary grade classroom based on early childhood principals. Identify the grade level and how many children are enrolled.

# CHAPTER IV

# DEVELOPING THE CURRICULUM

## Chapter Outline

- Role of the Teacher
- Role of the Administrator
- Different Kinds of Play
- Children's Needs
- Guidelines for Purchasing Materials
- Physical Environment
- Outdoor Area
- Program Evaluation
- Questions for Chapter IV

Designing Effective Early Childhood Environments

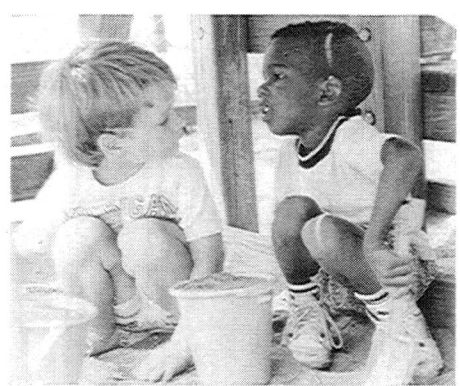
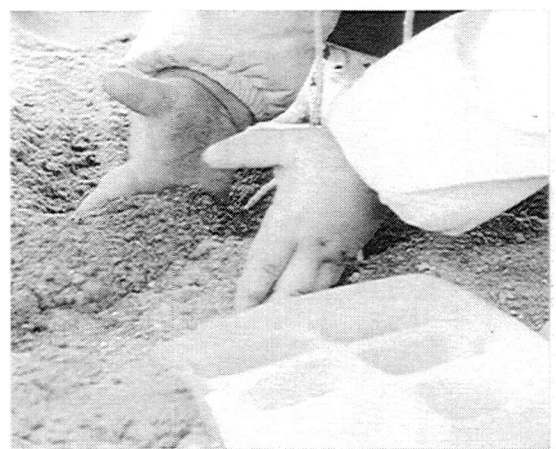
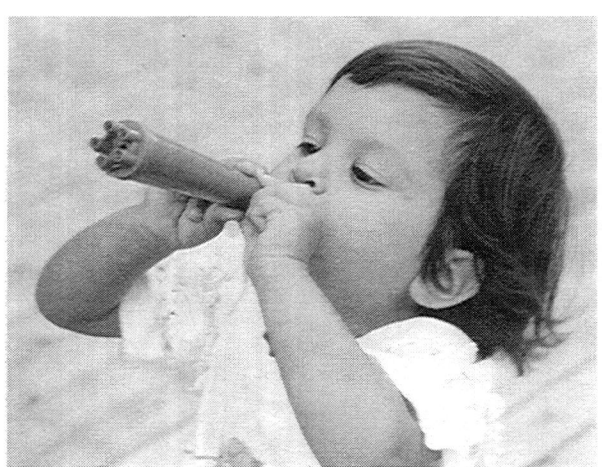

Photos copyright April S. Haase

# CHAPTER IV

# DEVELOPING THE CURRICULUM

All young children construct their learning through play. They learn by talking and messing around and using their five senses and four areas of development- cognitive, social/emotional, language and physical. Early childhood, defined by the National Association for the Education of Young Children (NAEYC) includes birth through eight years and the programs are for infants, toddlers, preschoolers and kindergarten through third grade in schools and their parents.

Teachers educated in play based curricula implement and facilitate effective learning environments for young children. Play must be valued by all the adults, especially those directly educating of the children. Quality programs provide for ample time and space to experiment, explore and manipulate the equipment and materials in the environment.

There is a delicate balance in the curriculum. Children need stimulation and new materials to investigate. However, the materials cannot be changed before the child has explored all the possibilities of the materials. A learning center that is the same, month after month, is quickly overlooked by children. Sometimes if a popular center is changed weekly, it limits the learning in the classroom. Teachers must be excellent observers of children and when interest wanes, add new items to the center, or move it to another area in the room. Watch the children. They will tell teachers when it is time to change the ecology of the classroom.

What is learned through play? Children construct their own reality of the world and learn life skills. Some of the skills are:

* Decision making
* Problem solving
* Creative thinking
* Learning comparisons
* Learning discriminations
* Making predictions
* Discovering cause and effect relationships
* Developing feelings and reactions
* Playing different roles

## Designing Effective Early Childhood Environments

* Identifying properties and qualities
* Constructing and learning functions
* Causing transformations
* Coordinating of information
* Having the excitement of invention
* Anticipating change
* Learning academic skills

Play develops every area of the child, but most of all, play makes learning fun and develops the basis for life long learning.

**Role of the Teacher**

The role of the teacher is to facilitate each child's development. The child is actively involved in constructing their own knowledge. The curriculum is a catalyst for concepts to be learned and sets limits for each child. That is, the child has certain choices in the learning process and the curriculum provides the boundaries. This is a different approach to learning than in most programs for young children in primary schools. In schools today, the teacher disseminates the information to be learned and directs all children in the process. Children in this environment are passive, extrinsic learners, while those involved in play are creative, intrinsic learners.

The teacher who is effective in a play based environment:

* Understands child development theory
* Is able to put theory into practice
* Constructs a hands on, play based curriculum
* Organizes the play environment
* Is flexible and able to accommodate to the needs of individual children
* Is an active observer and listener
* Interacts when needed
* Expands each child's learning
* Asks specific and general questions
* Evaluates self, child and the environment regularly
* Promotes change in self, child and environment regularly
* Has parents in classroom regularly
* Shares information with parents consistently

The teacher is the facilitator in a play based program. Rather than directing, the teacher guides activities in the classroom and selects appropriate materials and activities. The equipment must be durable, safe, easy to handle and accessible to children. The equipment should be adaptable to more than one use because budgets are almost always limited. Therefore, equipment and materials should be of high quality to keep replacement costs low.

Chapter 4: Developing the Curriculum

**Role of the Administrator**

What is the role of an administrator in early childhood programs? Administrators can support or undermine the learning in a play based program if the theory is not understood. It is important that administrators understand the theory of play and the practice in the classrooms. Just saying they support the program is not enough. Administrators establish credibility for the program by defending the curriculum and teachers to parents and the community at large. If they do not have a thorough understanding of the theory and practice of play based learning, the program is at risk.

Administrators who do not understand that young children learn differently than children in higher elementary grades, often can pressure teachers to "prove" children are learning. It is easier for administrators to support and defend academic programs with drill and practice lessons on specific skills that can be tested. Parents understand traditional learning and are comfortable when their children are taught using methods they experienced in school. Rote learning is easy to teach and if the development of young children is not understood, the test scores "prove" what the child is "learning." In actuality, the test scores only tell how the child is able to respond to traditional assessment and evaluation.

Teachers, however, who use play based curricula, need to establish evaluation procedures for each child and what is being learned in the curriculum. Teachers trained in techniques of observation must develop systematic record keeping methods to collect, record, assess and evaluate the information to "prove" to administrators and parents that children are learning specific skills and general knowledge, even though they are enjoying their learning. Teacher observations usually are a better source of information on each child than most standardized early childhood tests.

Administrators who play a crucial role in a play based program

* Study what a child learns in a play based program
* Support teachers trained in play
* Are wary of quiet, tidy classrooms
* Do not reward teachers who have quiet, neat classrooms
* Understand that children learn through talking, moving around, messing and combining materials in the environment
* Provide regular in service training for all staff
* Attend all training sessions
* Network with other administrators
* Invite other administrators to training sessions

## Different Kinds of Play

There are different kinds of play. Play is not just simply "playing around." As with most things in life, play is more complex than it appears. There is not one definition of what play is. That is why children, parents, teachers and administrators often talk about play, but mean different things. There are three categories of play in early childhood classrooms and depending on how the play materials are presented, most activities in the curriculum can be placed in one of three categories.

## Free Play

This is the highest most developed category of play, theoretically speaking. Children are in control of constructing their own learning through manipulating, exploring and experiencing their environment. There is almost no adult intervention; rather children construct what they need to know, students use the teacher as a resource and take as much time as they need to learn. The experimental Summer Hill School in England was based on free play.

## Guided Play

Guided play describes most of the curricula in early childhood classrooms. The teacher designs the environment and guides the child's learning. Activities in the curriculum are based on the interests of the children and they make decisions, problem solve and think creatively during the day. The time in the classroom can limit the learning process, however, and home activities are often suggested to parents to extend learning in the classroom. Selected activities rotate on a weekly or monthly basis and integrates learning in the cognitive, social/emotional, language and physical areas of the child.

## Directed Play

Directed Play is used in "academic" early childhood programs and is based on learning specific concepts and skills. It is usually an artificial play like setting. The teacher decides what the children need to learn, including unrelated facts and concepts. The child is an extrinsic learner with little autonomy or responsibility for learning. The curriculum is often learned by rote, drill and practice methods and evaluation is testing of facts and performance of tasks. Many of the academic curricula are in series and published by text book companies. This method of teaching is used in primary grades in elementary schools, but frequently is in preschools that "prepare" children for school.

Chapter 4: Developing the Curriculum

**Children's Needs**

Young children in order to be active learners and develop a firm base for life-long learning need:

1. Time to explore, investigate and manipulate the environment
2. Privacy for play
3. Enough space to play, mess, move and talk
4. Numerous appropriate open ended materials
5. Adult interaction, not control
6. Assistance until they are able to make choices
7. A curriculum centering on their interests and abilities
8. Multicultural and nonsexist experiences and materials
9. Permission to refuse to participate in group activities
10. Clear, consistent limits on behavior
11. To have parents involved in their education
12. To be treated with dignity

Suggestions for teachers in play based classrooms

1. Limit rules for play during free time
2. Rotate a wide variety of materials regularly
3. Have many props for make believe play
4. Encourage children to control their own behaviors
5. Develop excellent observational skills
6. Be an active listener, not participant
7. Don't reward play with a payoff or reward
8. Do not make the classroom competitive

Remember, play does not have a product, rather it the process of how young children learn.


**Guidelines for Purchasing Materials**

Children learn through a wide range of experiences in the classroom. They need toys and materials that allow them to explore, experience and manipulate in order to learn about their world. Effective classrooms have a wide range of materials and activities accessible to children throughout the day. Many different kind of materials in each of the following categories are needed in order to develop the young child. They are:

**Sensory Materials** are needed to develop the five senses. Water, sand, clay, paint, air, wood and music are some mediums that are used for sensory development. Provide a wide range of materials to use with each medium to extend the learning, such as musical instruments to explore sounds. It is important to allow children to use "real" items they are familiar with and to learn safety rules. Children learn independence and develop autonomy when they are able to plan and implement their own learning, according to their needs and abilities.

**Manipulative Materials** develop hand-eye coordination skills, critical for reading and writing. Include, but do not limit materials to beads, puzzles, pegboards and lacing cards and other fine motor activities. Provide many opportunities for playing with manipulatives during the day at many centers.

**Gross Motor Equipment** such as climbing equipment, tires, slides, rocking toys, stairs and riding toys are examples of equipment needed to develop physical abilities. Children learn through movement. It is important they are given opportunities to develop their bodies, as well as their minds.

**Construction Materials** such as blocks, blocks and more blocks are the best value for the money because math and science concepts are learned through construction. Have many blocks available, so children have enough to construct large, detailed items with themes. Purchase a variety of blocks: large, small, irregular shaped, plastic, interlocking, cardboard and hardwood. Always purchase hardwood blocks, rather than pine for durability. Blocks are a popular item and need to be high quality in order to with stand constant use. **This is no place to save money.** Blocks are too expensive to constantly replace, rather buy high quality blocks and use the budget to expand the variety.

**Woodworking Materials** are also needed. Children need to learn how to safely use real tools, not toys. Hammers, nails, saws and goggles are needed. Soft wood, styrofoam and pumpkins can be used for hammering to develop good hand eye coordination. Make sure an adult is assigned to this area as a safety precaution.

**Computers in the Classroom** are not a new idea. The age of technology is now in the classroom. The question whether we should have a computer was answered almost a decade ago. In 1980, 35,000 computers were sold. Three years later, 3,500,000 computers were delivered and sold not only to businesses, but also to schools and parents for home use. Today, there is hardly a school system that has not integrated technology into all levels of education, including preschool. Children are as comfortable today with computers as we were with radios yesterday.

Remember, however, computers are only a tool for learning. When teachers use computers they should apply good curriculum principles to computer activities. There are three areas for the educational use of computers.

1. Creative applications as in music and art
2. Word processing
3. Mathematics

Seymour Papert (1980), developer of the Logo language and Professor at Massachusetts Institute of Technology, suggests in order for the computer to be an effective learning tool, the child must be in control of the computer, NOT vice versa.

# Chapter 4: Developing the Curriculum

By programming the computer, Papert says, "children acquire a sense of mastery over the piece of the most modern and powerful technology and establish an intimate contact with some of the deepest ideas from science, from mathematics and from the art of intellectual building."

At what age should children be introduced to the computer? Many preschoolers already are familiar with them and some have the machines in their homes. So this is a moot question. The microcomputer, as television before it, is viewed as a medium that invites social isolation. If software is selected carefully and children are encouraged to problem solve together using the computer as a tool, this is unlikely to happen.

Six questions to ask when purchasing software for young children were developed by Warren Buckleitner, of the High/Scope Educational Research Foundation. They are:

1. Is the software easy to use?
2. Is the software interactive?
3. Is the software child proof?
4. Is there a strong curriculum content?
5. Is there enough novelty in the program?
6. Can the software be changed for individual children?

## Physical Environment

The physical environment can be difficult to design to meet the needs of young children in care. Even when a building is designed and built to specifications, or renovated, it is rarely a perfect setting. If possible, child care facilities should be on the ground floor. This is easier for parents, children and staff. The rooms need to be large enough for active play, but have a floor plan to avoid safety hazards, such as running in open spaces.

Fifty square feet per child is preferable when calculating the space needed in a center, although most licensing requirements call for only 35 square feet of usable space per child. Divide larger rooms into curriculum areas such as blocks, language arts, art, housekeeping, work bench, science and math, music, movement, water and sand play, social studies, nap, computer and library. Use smaller rooms for specialized activities or more quiet, individualized time.

Use dividers, equipment and partitions to section off areas of the room. Elevated platforms, used as a stage or lofts for reading or quiet play with storage space or play space underneath, increases the usable square footage in smaller rooms. Clearly define interest areas with signs hung over each area describing the skills learned by the children. Change smaller signs to describe specific skills learned in the changing activities within centers.

## Designing Effective Early Childhood Environments

Equipment is expensive, so invest in high quality hardwood equipment and keep replacement costs low. Centers going out of business and public schools are a good source of high quality furniture. Buy equipment that is attractive and has ample storage and display space to avoid clutter. Children need access to materials such as paint, paper, clay and crayons on a daily basis. Limit the number of things on the shelf so the child can make decisions. Rotate the available materials on a regular basis.

The size of the kitchen areas and the equipment depends on the frequency of meals and snacks served. Toilet and handwashing facilities should be child sized and available at all times to children and easy to clean and disinfect. Also include an entry/exit area for parents and children; nap area, faculty lounge and rest area for ill children.

When designing a room arrangement locate the water source in the room and designate that area "W" for the wet area. Opposite the wet area, at the other end of the room place the "D" area or dry area. On the left, label the room "Q" for quiet area and the opposite side "N" for noisy. The plan should look like this.

W(Wet) Area

| Q(Quiet) Area | N(Noisy) Area |
|---|---|

D(Dry) Area

Now fill in the activities in each quadrant of a classroom. Name activities in the noisy-wet area, noisy-dry area, dry-quiet area and quiet-wet area. This is a beginning rough draft. Now fill in the needed equipment, such as furniture and materials. Supplies are consumable and do not need to be listed.

Chapter 4: Developing the Curriculum

**Outdoor Area**

Outdoor areas are designed with activity areas, similar to those in the classrooms. For example, large scale painting, large muscle activities, water and sand play, socio-dramatic play, housekeeping, music, creative movement and story telling are fun outside under the trees. Unless there is a weather alert, children should spend some time outside **everyday**. The play area should be fenced with a four foot fence and be close or adjacent to the child care facility. At least 1200 square feet in programs with five or more children is the minimum space allowed in many states.

There are few, if any, regulations for the safety of outdoor equipment. Be wary of climbing equipment that can only be used for one purpose. Rather new structures should encourage fantasy play, in addition to gross motor exercise. Be careful of sharp edges, metal pieces that rust, unsturdy or oversized pieces of equipment. Talking with other professionals and attending workshops on outside play environments can identify corporations or individuals who construct appropriate, safe and inviting outdoor environments. Store equipment outside on the playground in sheds or garages with wide doors and child proof locks.

**Program Evaluation**

Formative evaluations of programs should be completed annually by the administrator of the program. The formative evaluation measures the progress made toward goals and objectives defined by the staff and board the prior year. After completing the evaluation, new goals and objectives are set for the coming fiscal year. Four steps to follow in the evaluation process are:

1. State the goals and objectives of the program clearly.
2. Spend time with each employee and small groups of parents to evaluate objectives.
3. Write a concise report, for employees, board members and parents.
4. Disseminate information on the program to those listed above and specific community organizations and local schools.

Specifically, administrators preparing the evaluation report should:

* Use common sense when organizing the task. Keep the language concise and the length as brief as possible.
* Outline each section of the report (goals, objectives met, objectives still to be met, evaluation, identification of new goals and objectives for the coming year).
* State philosophy, goals and objectives of program as related to children, parents, staff and community.
* Use graphs to describe data.
* Use case studies when appropriate (with no names of course).

Designing Effective Early Childhood Environments

* Identify needed changes and the implementation as short or long term goals.
* Write the report in short, easy to understand paragraphs and sentences.
* Disseminate reports on time.

# Questions for Chapter IV

1. Choose an existing early childhood classroom and draw the floor plan. Then, draw a second plan based on information in this chapter. Describe and justify the suggested changes.

2. Interview three early childhood teachers (preschool program, kinder garten and primary grade) on how they would change the environ ment if funds were not an issue.

3. Interview an administrator if an early childhood program and ask what changes could be made in the program.

# CHAPTER V

# SUGGESTED EQUIPMENT FOR EARLY CHILDHOOD ENVIRONMENTS

## Chapter Outline

- Early Childhood Classroom Equipment
- Room Arrangements -- Preschool and Kindergarten
- Room Arrangements -- Primary Grades
- Methods of Learning
- Summary

## DRAFTSMAN'S EASLES

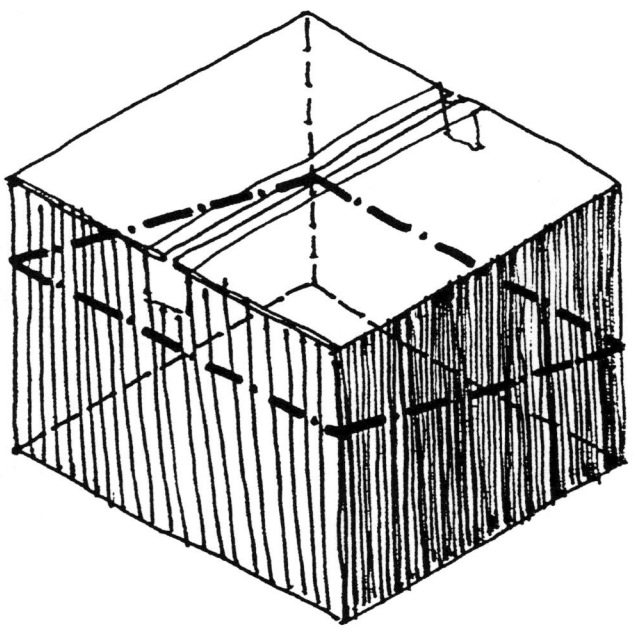

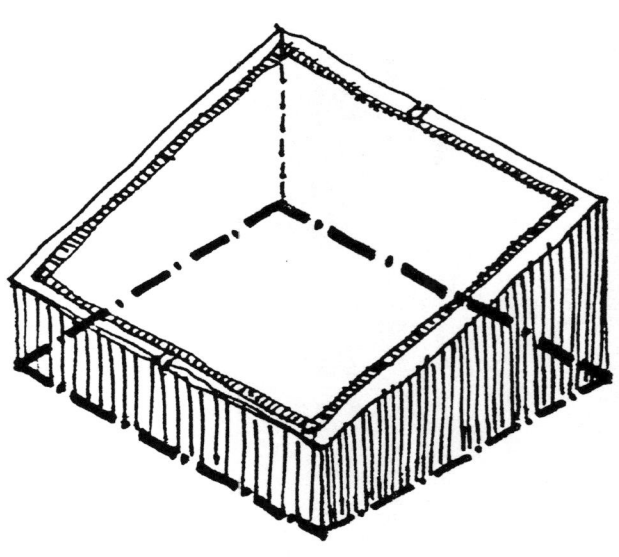

# CHAPTER V
# Equipment to Construct for Early Childhood Environments

## Early Childhood Classroom Equipment

## Draftsman's Easels

A writing/drawing area is part of every early childhood classroom. A variety of interesting and inviting materials are found here. They can include a table with chairs for two or three children, an easel area, a typewriter, a floor area, clip boards hanging in many places in the room to keep "grocery lists" or to write "letters." The draftsman's easel is a unique addition to this area. It gives another perspective to writing and introduces different tools of the craft.

These easels are easy to make. Reinforce the end of a cardboard box and cut off the end section as illustrated. A piece of poster board taped to the writing surface makes a smooth area on which to draw. Papers can be held by push pins or tape.

**AREAS OF LEARNING**

### Motor Skills

* Laterality, or knowing that two sides of the body are different from each other, is explored when the child holds a tool with one hand and draws with the other. Young children manipulate only the writing utensils at first. Then finally they try to prop a tool (ruler or compass) with one hand and draw with the other.

* Young children do not understand left to right progression but after practice, begin to draw from the top down and at last from side to side. The sides--all sides--are explored first and then laterality is discovered. This is basic in developing reading skills.

* Fine motor coordination is increased as children manipulate writing and drawing materials and practice.

* Spatial awareness is increased as the child realizes the boundaries of the easel and how to place objects on the paper.

* Directionality is learned with top to bottom and left to right progressions.

*Designing Effective Early Childhood Environments*

   * Midline is crossed with the use of rulers or exploring top to bottom, left to right.

**Language Skills**

   * Tools of a draftsman include rulers, templates, straight edge, table stencils, compass and pencils, all new words to be learned.

   * Designs created are labeled lines, angles, and shapes.

   * Children describe their drawings, explain their strategies and discuss with each other possible extensions.

   * Writing about the creation can be a natural inclusion and appropriate addition.

**Emotional Skills**

   * This is usually an individual activity and adds an opportunity for privacy during the day.

   * Easels are inviting to children who avoid or shy away from other writing areas. The tools appeal to children and draws them to this activity.

**Social Skills**

   * Taking turns with two or three easels provides an opportunity to learn to share.

   * Side by side easels invite conversation when children share tools, give suggestions or discuss their creations.

**Extension of Learning**

   * Many different materials can be used with these easels such as rulers, pencils, erasers, compasses, templates, markers, pens, various colors of paper, colored pencils and wallpaper.

# String Snap Board

This activity is a lot of fun, but messy and requires a teacher to be in the area. The String Snap Board provides a different way of painting and should be set up where the clean up is easy and then stored for future use.

A 2"x4" piece of wood with several nails partially embedded is clamped to a narrow table. String or yarn is attached to the nails and trays of paint lie along side the 2"x4" board. See illustration. Paper, on a raised surface, is placed on the opposite side from the paint. The string is placed in some paint, pulled taut and snapped to create a splattered line design.

# STRING SNAP BOARD

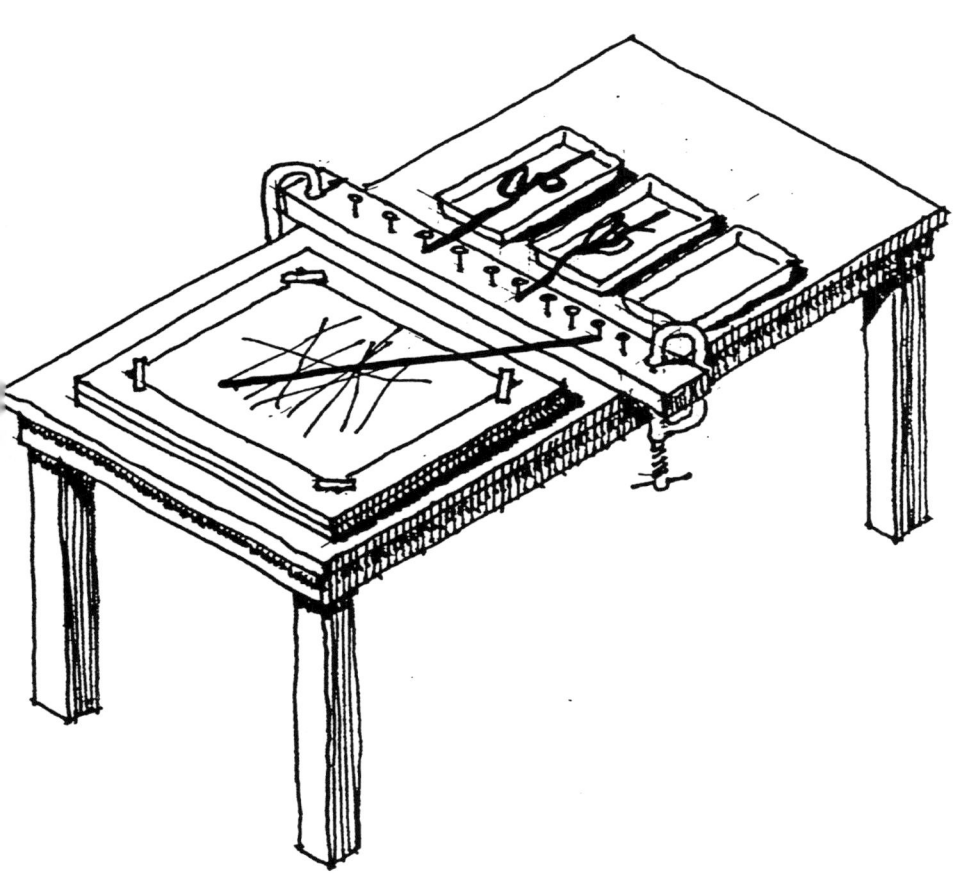

## AREAS OF LEARNING

### Motor Skills

* Eye-hand coordination is strengthened when the string is clasped or pinched and then let go.
* Tension is felt in the arm muscles when pulling up on the string.
* There is an understanding of the direction "up" because the string must be pulled up to work.
* The child traces where the string landed by its print.
* The print shows that a taut line produces a straight line.
* The child feels the effect of force and tension on the string. Cause and effect are learned when the harder the string is pulled, the stronger the print appears and there is more of a splatter of paint.

### Language Skills

* The structure itself has new vocabulary such as nails, 2x4, C-clamp, paint colors and paint trays.
* Descriptive words are also explored such as snap, taut and print.
* Action words which are part of this activity include pull, let go, higher, harder, hold, pinch, etc.

### Emotional Skills

* For a three year old, there is an element of surprise when the paint splatters all over.
* The four year olds are strong and pull hard. This is a release of tension and shows off their newly found strength.
* Fives are more cautious but also are more creative and precise in where they want the string to go and where they want to place the paper.
* This is fun and always successful. No two "prints" come out alike.

### Social Skills

* Because this activity is so much fun, taking turns is usually not a problem.
* Children encourage others to do it and help decide what colors to use.
* This is a great one on one time for the child and teacher.

### Extension of Learning

* Wear smocks!!

* Vary the lengths of the string, the thickness of the strings and the consistency of the paint.

* A dry material such as chalk dust can be used instead of paint.

* This snap board can be attached to the end of a water table or any other narrow table.

# Raised Platform

A raised platform is designed to give more space. It gives two levels in a corner of the room. Underneath is a low area into which adults cannot enter, so it is truly a child's domain. When two or three children enter the area, they usually take pillows and books with them. Other materials could be stored underneath. Avoid getting the area too cluttered. When the children are on top of the platform, there is more opportunity for eye to eye contact with adults and the children get a different perspective on the environment.

The top is framed with 2"x4" boards and a piece of three-fourths inch plywood completes the top. The legs are 4"x4" posts or two 2"x4" boards bolted together. These posts are bolted to the frame and then the top, sides and legs are all carpeted.

### AREAS OF LEARNING

### Motor Skills

* The platform provides for climbing and using large muscles for gross motor coordination.

* Jumping from the platform or dropping bean bags or toys helps the child experience gravity, force and distance.

* Visual perception is needed to see the distance from the top to the floor.

* Spatial and body awareness are tested when the child realizes how the body needs to function to compensate for the space above and below the platform.

* Crawling and creeping are also enhanced.

### Language Skills

* Use words identifying positions such as: top, bottom, up, down, side, under, beneath, underneath, around, next to, on, off, lean.

* When more than one child plays at a time many communication skills are acquired through play in this area.

# RAISED PLATFORM

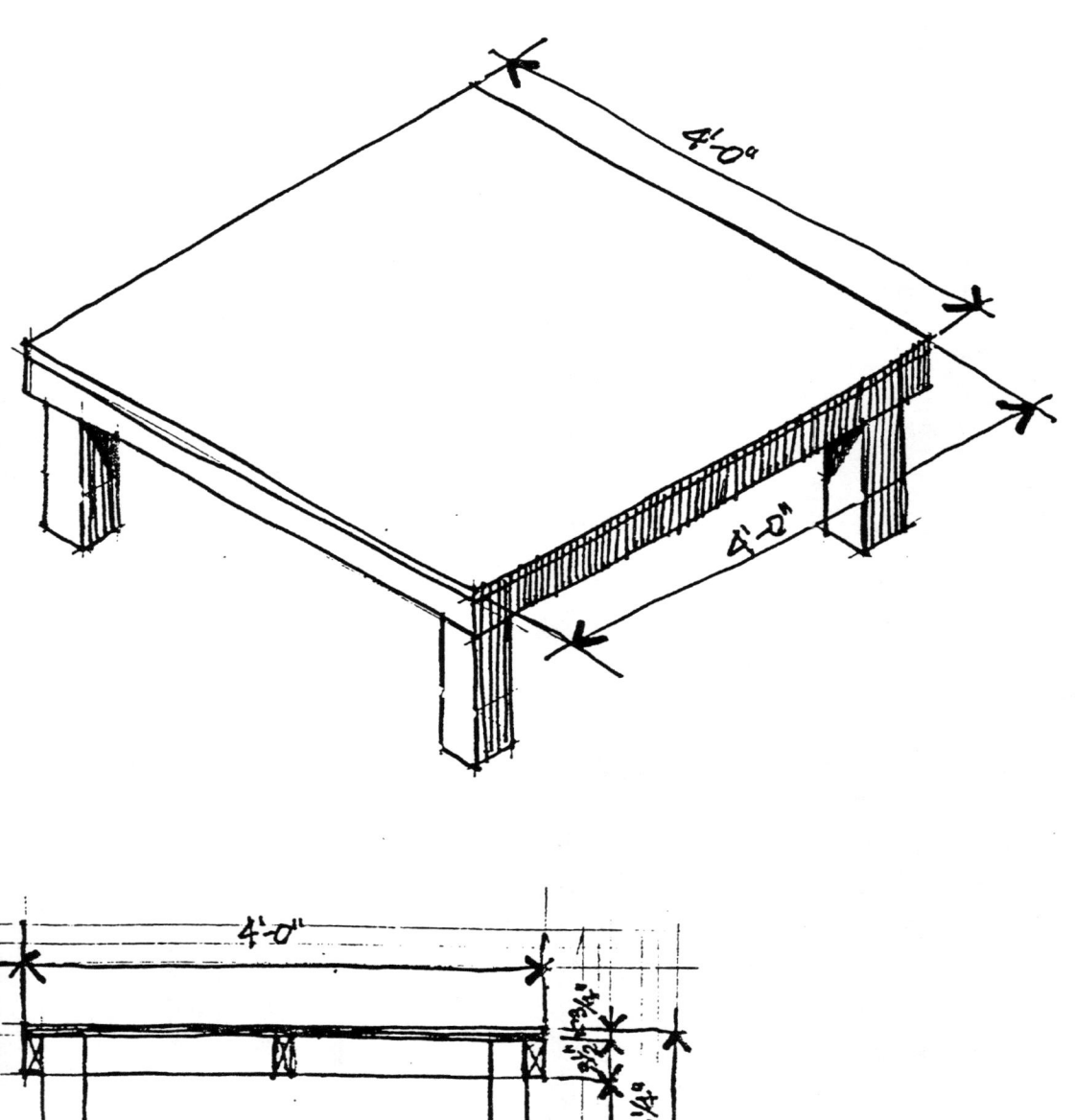

SECTION

Chapter 5: Suggested Equipment for Early Childhood Environments

* If blocks are added, then classification and sorting language is developed, while dolls or dress ups add different vocabulary.

**Emotional Benefits**

* Children reveal relationships, fears and feelings in movement. (Fleming, 1968) Imagination and creativity develop when a child acts out frustrations, joys or questions about life.

* Development of physical skills makes a child feel competent. Adults who encourage children to act under their own power and control such as running, climbing, throwing or cutting with scissors allows a child to develop in all four areas: cognitive, social/emotional, physical and language.

* This platform provides another privacy place.

**Social Advantages**

* This platform is big enough for more than one child. Parallel play can occur, but probably more social play occurs than solitary play on this platform. The superhero play on this platform resembles Follow the Leader. Children jump off, slide under, yell who is after them and climb to the top, again and again.

* Along with practice play, symbolic play occurs when dolls are added and the children "feed" the babies or they set up "house."

* Simple games occur from the platform such as taking turns jumping or tossing a ball to another person.

**Suggestions**

* Blankets are great for creating a tent.

* The structure is relatively light and can be pulled away from the wall. This creates new spaces and different kinds of play.

* Just about any toy or sociodramatic prop can be added to enhance the learning in this area.

# Block Shelves

The importance of blocks in an early childhood program is stressed earlier in this text. These shelves provide an easy way to store them when the shape of the block is taped to the shelf where it belongs. Children match the block to the shape and easily group like-blocks together.

This unit can be made with 1"x10" boards for the sides, top and shelves. One-quarter inch masonite can be attached to form the back.

Designing Effective Early Childhood Environments

# BLOCK SHELVES

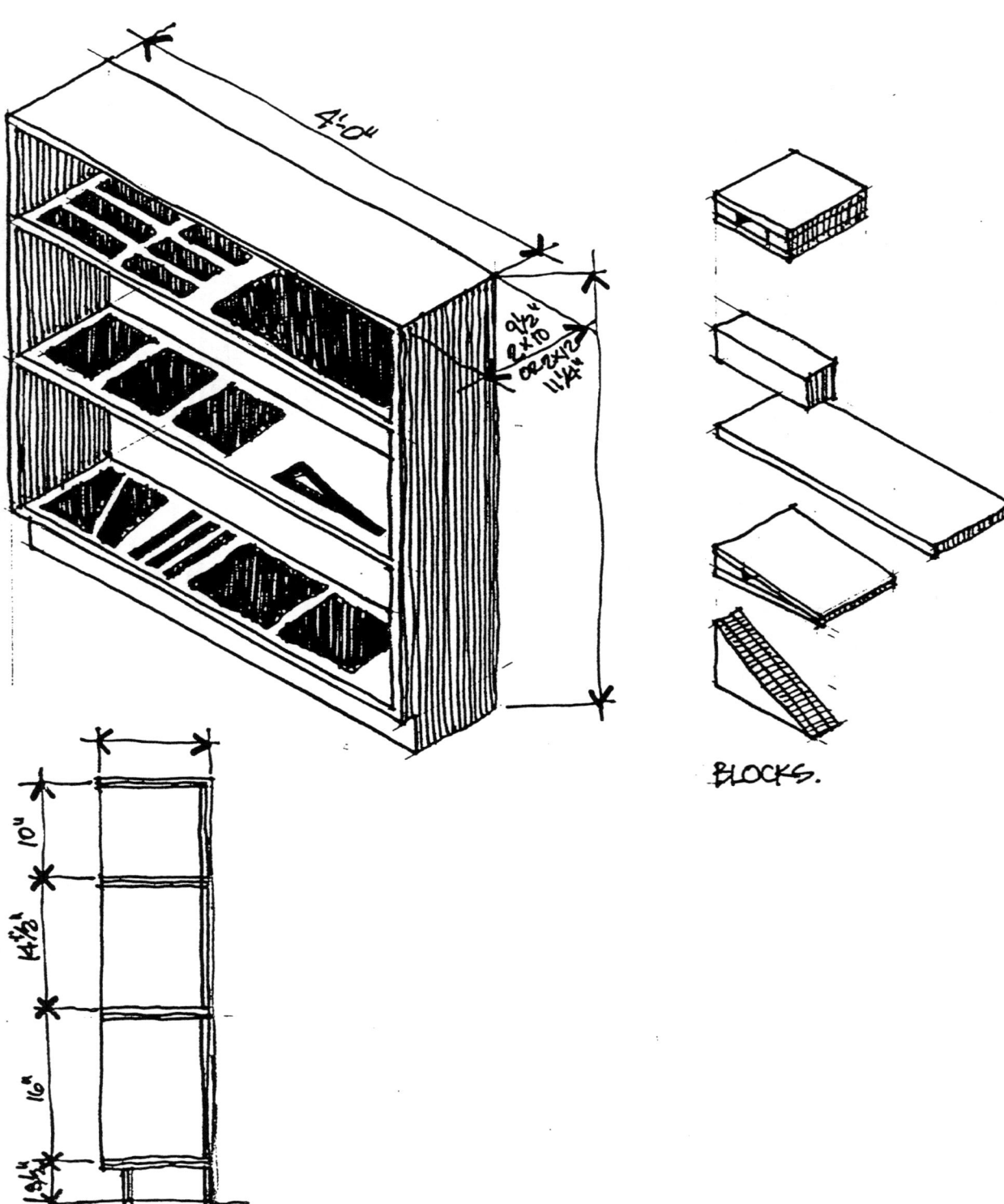

BLOCKS.

Chapter 5: Suggested Equipment for Early Childhood Environments

## AREAS OF LEARNING

### Motor Skills

* Balance, gravity, eye-hand coordination and depth perception are skills enhanced through block building.

### Language Skills

* Shapes of blocks are identified as the children label their structures.

* Spatial words such as top, bottom, back, front, side, around, beside and under are all experienced.

### Emotional Skills

* Children show pride in building and also release energy in building and knocking the blocks down.

* Blocks help children exercise their powers, muscles and imagination.

* Children learn their limits from manipulating these blocks and exercise their developing concepts of volume, area and structural support.

### Social Skills

* Blocks usually involve two or more children working together with a goal and objectives.

* Dress up clothes brought into this area add new themes to dramatic play, such as spaceships, airplanes, airports, cages, zoos, department stores and barns.

* Primary grade children profit from the manipulation of blocks. Thinking and problem solving skills, mathematical concepts, classification, and observation are all developed through the use of blocks.

### Suggestions

* After children explore the properties of the blocks, put tape on the floor to form a pathway or have large cards with designs for children to match the blocks to the pattern. The blocks can also be a walkway from one area to another.

* Small plastic people and cars can be added to the block area. Girls in the classroom tend to play in the block area when props are added.

* Remember, blocks are not off limits to teachers. In fact a study by Day and Sheehan (1974) stated the more teacher/child interaction there is, the more cooperation and mutual respect are developed in children.

# Manipulative Shelves

These shelves hold bins or small plastic tubs, each containing a separate toy or manipulative. Put the shelves on wheels for easy moving. A good varnish or glossy paint will keep the shelves from splintering on the edges and make them easier to clean. Glue picture labels of each toy or manipulative to the bin and the place on the shelf. For older children, use pictures and words on the bins and shelves. Divisions help children focus better on the desired item.

## AREAS OF LEARNING

**Motor Skills**

* Fine motor coordination is developed.
* Figure ground is developed when the child finds the place for toy on the shelf.
* Perception of forms is developed. Cards showing a pattern of beads on a string can be included. Children reproduce the sequence.
* One to one correspondence is emphasized through pegs and buttons.

**Language Skills**

* Labels help with language development.
* Use words that pertain to manipulation such as in, out, on, together, done, finished, pull, and push.

**Emotional Skills**

* There is a sense of success when the manipulative is used and returned to the proper place.
* Toys with many pieces can be challenging, but must be developmentally appropriate. If there are too many pieces, younger children will dump or abandon the toy.
* Manipulatives are good for solitary or small group play.

**Social Skills**

* Manipulatives are solitary toys and provide a feeling of success to the individual.
* Sharing of the manipulatives occur and children help each other find needed pieces.

Chapter 5: Suggested Equipment for Early Childhood Environments

## MANIPULATIVE SHELVES

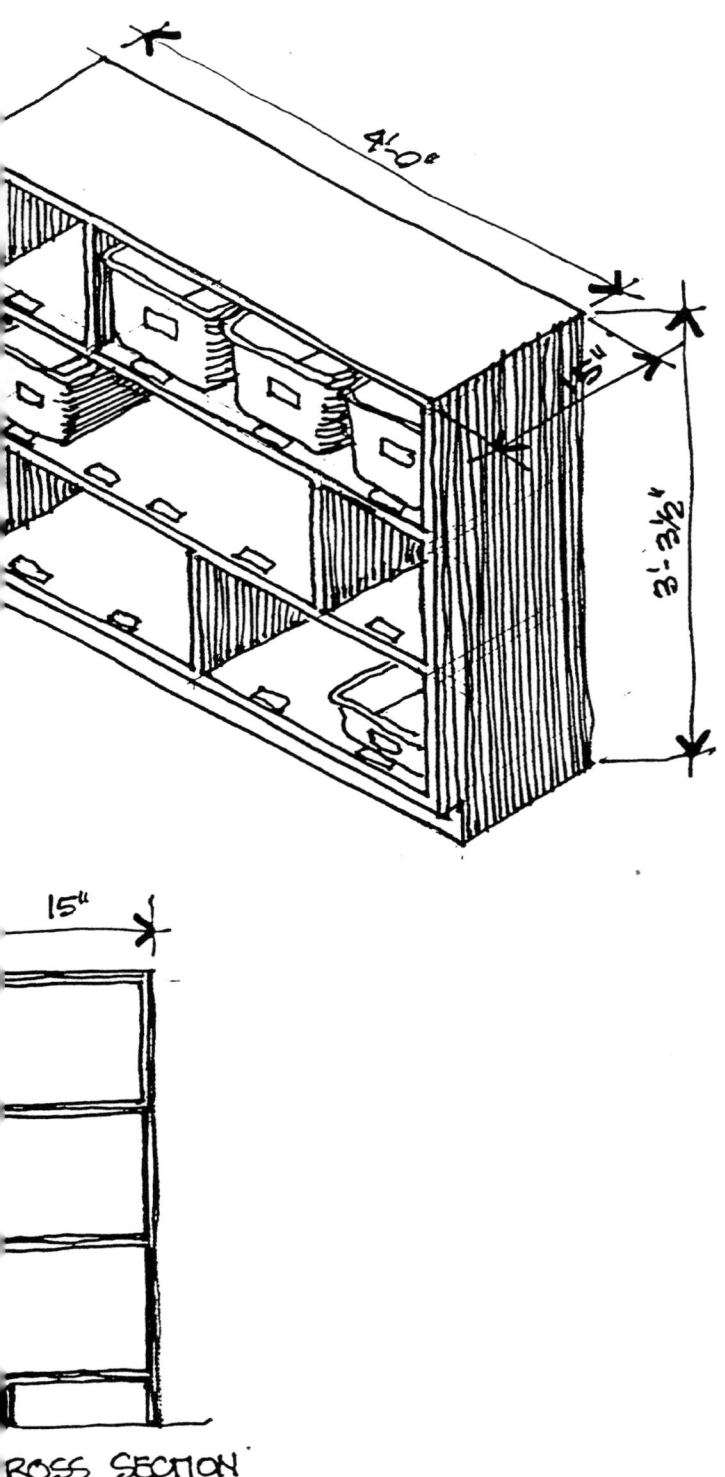

CROSS SECTION

### Suggestions

* If there is a large number of manipulatives and children, the teacher should have two shelving units in two different areas of the room to allow ample space for exploration.

* Soft plastic kitchen sink tubs that come in a variety of colors work well for storing manipulatives such as wooden pegs, plastic pegs, Legos, buttons, stringing beads, plastic blocks, Lincoln Logs, wooden trains, small wooden blocks and geoboards.

Puzzle Shelf

A puzzle shelf is neat and inviting, not cluttered and ignored. The shelf should be open and organized. All parts of the shelving need to be intact and free from splinters or sharp edges. Display puzzles side by side as opposed to stacking. When puzzles are stacked children dump puzzles, do not return the puzzles, lose pieces and lose interest in them. Children need puzzles for success in solving problems. Children solve problems by looking for clues in the puzzles and playing around with the clues to solve the problem.

Puzzles can be color coded for difficulty by marking their containers with various colors of masking tape, e.g. red=easy, blue=more difficult, yellow= most difficult. Children can challenge themselves according to how much they feel like pursuing in a given day. The shelf unit is made of plywood with a nontoxic paint or a finished wood with a nontoxic coat of varnish. Shelves can be slanted for better visibility of the puzzles or lay flat. Either way, a small lip at the front of the shelf lessens the chance of puzzles falling off the shelves. This unit could be made larger or smaller depending upon the needs of the user.

## AREAS OF LEARNING

### Motor Skills

* Developing perception of forms. Puzzles encourage children to make comparisons and constructive guesses.

* Visual sequencing occurs as the child reproduces a set or puzzle and repeats it.

* Puzzles enhance figure ground development when a needed piece is selected from the others.

* Fine motor coordination is developed.

* Include some puzzles with knobs. Grasping the knob gives further practice in fine motor coordination.

Chapter 5: Suggested Equipment for Early Childhood Environments

## PUZZLE SHELF

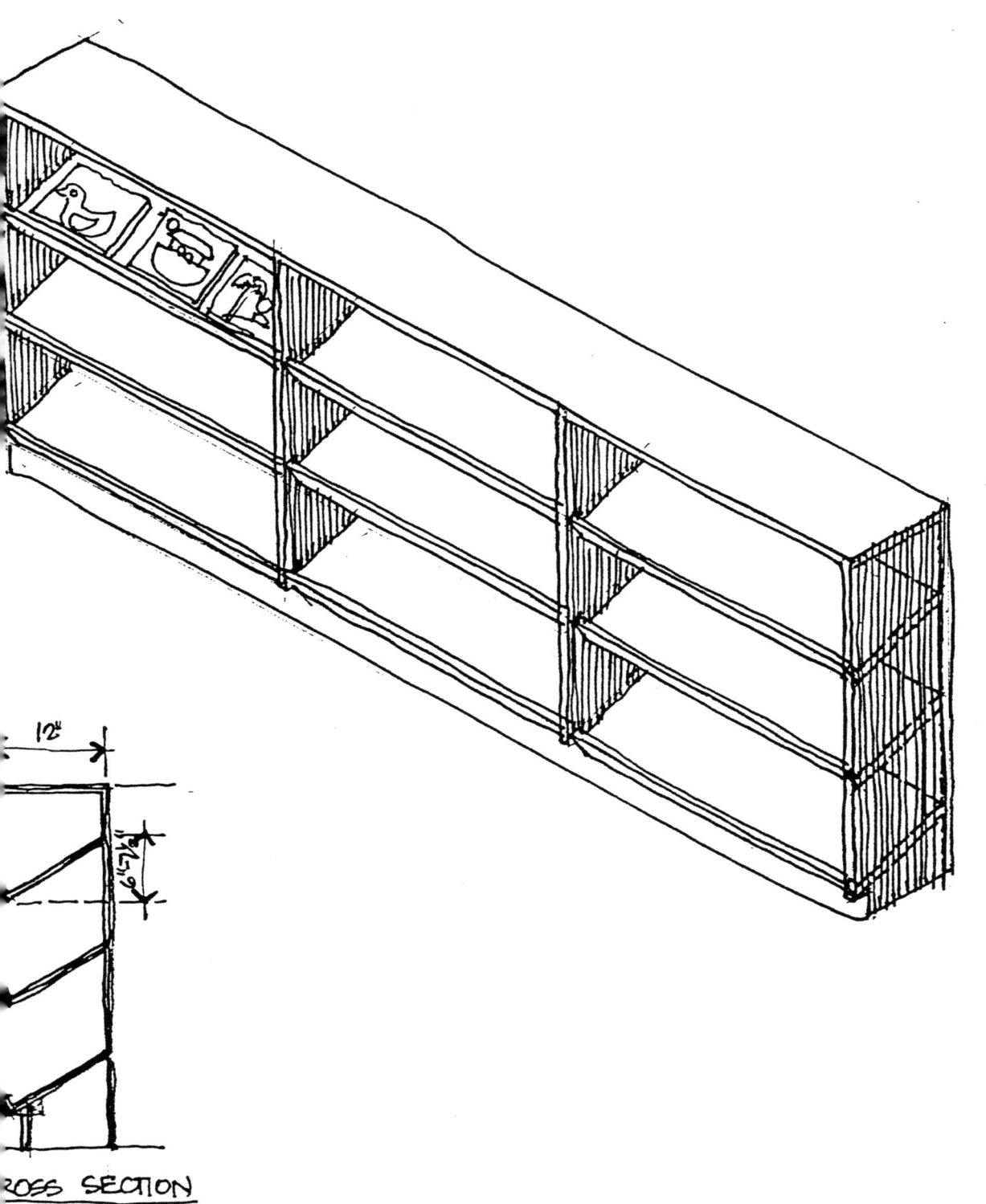

CROSS SECTION

* Closure is experienced when the puzzle is completed.

* Discrimination abilities are developed by tactile manipulation and visual perceptions in defining shape, color, texture, matching and pairing. (Mante and Mathisen, 1977)

* Puzzles present problems to be solved and the child uses all of his senses to accomplish that task. (Sylva, Brunner and Genova, 1976)

* Primary grade children are challenged by puzzles and especially enjoy the 100, 500 or even 1,000 piece variety.

**Language Skills**

* Terms are learned such as turn, over, flip, slide, in, out and push.

* Labels or new vocabulary are developed as the child identifies pictures or shapes of a puzzle.

* The scene depicted can be discussed and content information derived.

**Emotional Skills**

* A finished puzzle shows completeness and provides a feeling of success to the child.

* Children need a sense of closure and puzzles to achieve this feeling.

* Success is achieved when the puzzle is completed and correctly placed on the shelf.

**Social Skills**

* Sometimes children do puzzles cooperatively and take turns inserting the pieces.

* Large floor puzzles need cooperation and discussion by the group.

**Suggestions**

* Have a variety of puzzles including those with four pieces to 100 pieces, knobbed, foam rubber, wooden and cardboard puzzles.

* Do not display too many puzzles at one time. Rotation is better and more inviting.

# Storage Cubby

This unit is designed to maximize the useable space in the classroom. It provides for both storage of teacher's materials and a play area. The storage area above is easily reached by the teacher and the space below is easily accessible for individual play or space for two or three children.

Chapter 5: Suggested Equipment for Early Childhood Environments

## STORAGE CUBBY

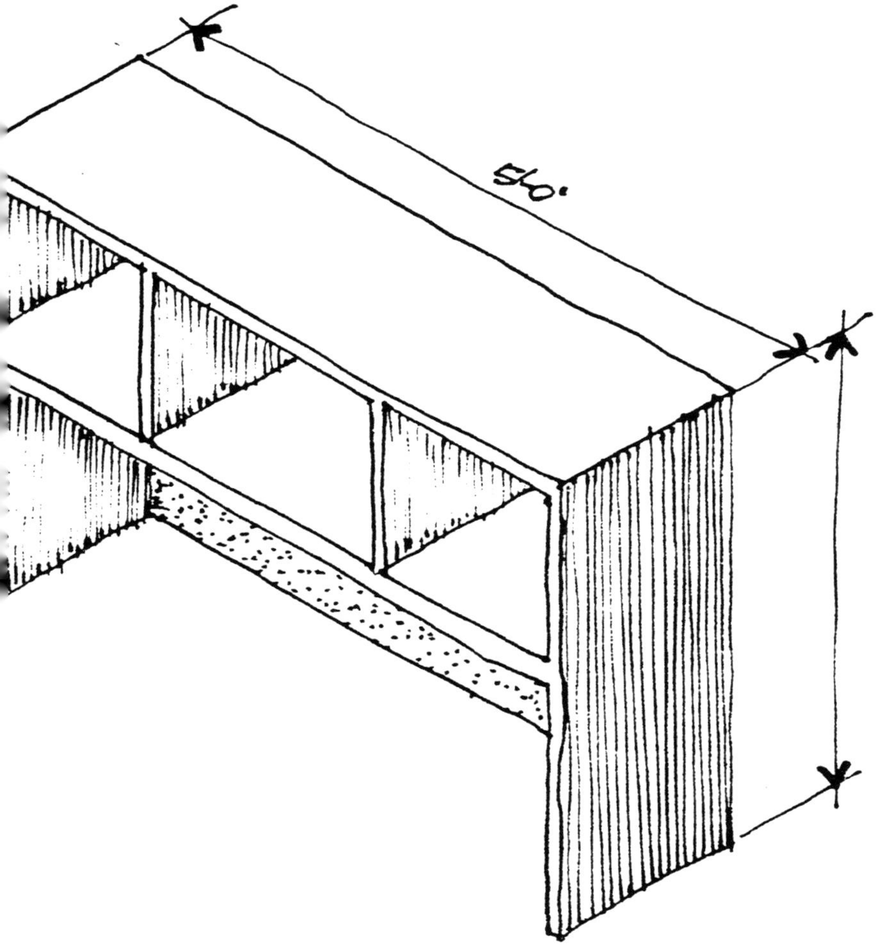

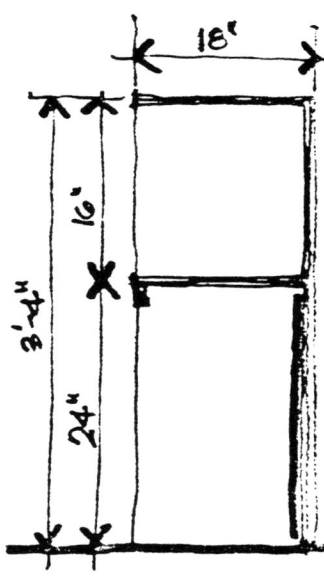

Designing Effective Early Childhood Environments

The storage section has any number of compartments. The area below can have a flannel board section, a board for magnets, a mirror and carpeting. The unit is made of three-fourths inch plywood and wood screws, plus any other fabrics or textures desired.

## AREAS OF LEARNING

**Motor Skills**

* Eye-hand coordination is strengthened.
* Body awareness is increased with a mirror.
* Shapes, colors and textures are explored, developing visual and tactile discrimination skills.
* The "secrets" of magnets are discovered.
* Spatial awareness is tested when the child works within the space provided.

**Language Skills**

* The vocabulary of shapes, colors and textures are learned, such as under, next to, big, little, stick, fall, drop, short and long.
* The mirror provides a "person" to talk to.

**Emotional Skills**

* A child has private space away from the main activity and noise in the classroom. It offers an opportunity to take time out and rejoin the group later.

**Social Skills**

* Children learn to share materials.
* Children learn to discuss ideas in a group.

# Steps

Before a child can learn addition and subtraction, the child must know on a physical level how to put things together and then reverse or take things apart. Steps can help with this.

Steps and ladders present opportunities to tactually explore concepts that young children cannot understand until the age of seven or eight. Some children get up to the top of a piece of equipment and panic because they cannot reverse their actions and get down. Smaller steps allow a child to be successful.

Chapter 5: Suggested Equipment for Early Childhood Environments

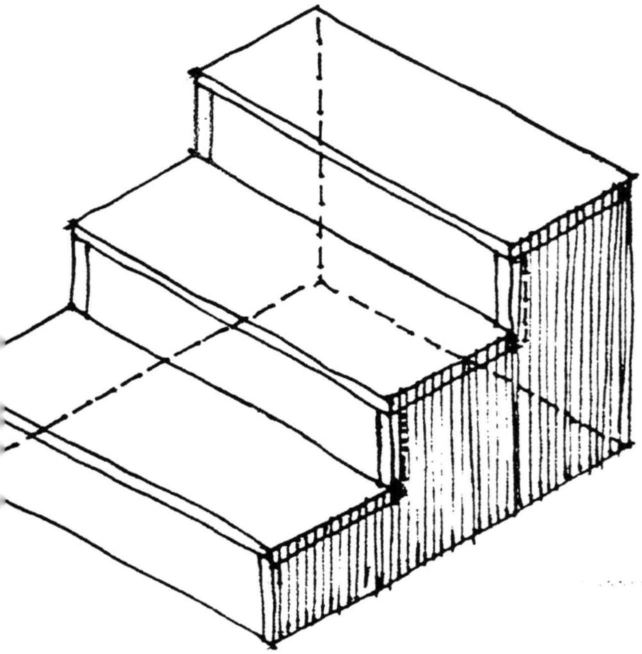

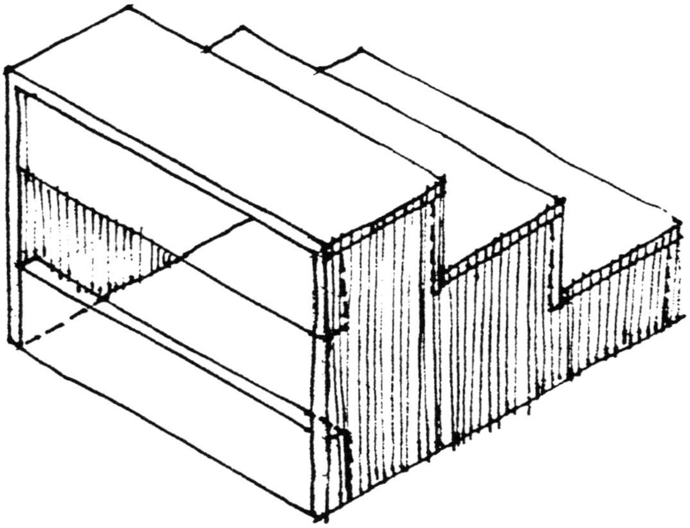

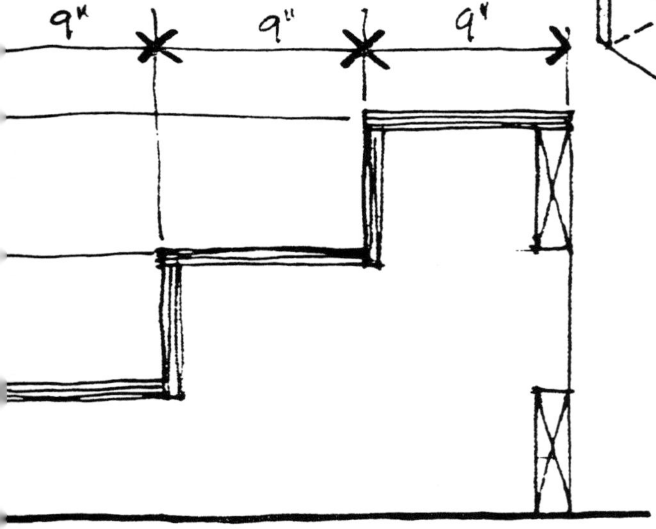

9" 9" 9"

65

Designing Effective Early Childhood Environments

## AREAS OF LEARNING

### Motor Skills

* Gross motor coordination and eye-foot coordination is enhanced.
* Body awareness is developed.
* Understand the physical strength needed to get up and down.
* Spatial awareness is strengthened.
* Balance is developed.

### Language Skills

* Spatial or relationship words include up, down, over, next to, top, bottom, high, low, climb and jump. These words all need a reference point--the child. (Kephart, 1975)

### Emotional Skills

* Steps are inviting and challenging.
* Steps are in the daily lives of children.

### Social Skills

* Children learn to take turns going up and down the steps.
* When music is added, other interactions evolve.
* Steps can be used next to a raised platform for climbing into a "space ship" or other sociodramatic play activity.
* Steps encourage jumping games.

### Suggestion

* Place a plank between the two steps to make a wider balance beam for younger children. Be sure it is no higher than they are tall.

# Balance Beam

Early childhood programs must have a balance beam or at least one made out of a line of unit blocks. The drawing shows a simple and inexpensive way to build a balance beam. The support pieces are made with 2"x10" boards cut to the measurements shown in the drawing. A 2"x4" board, sanded and varnished, creates the beam for balancing activities. This structure can easily be stored out of sight.

Chapter 5: Suggested Equipment for Early Childhood Environments

## BALANCE BEAM

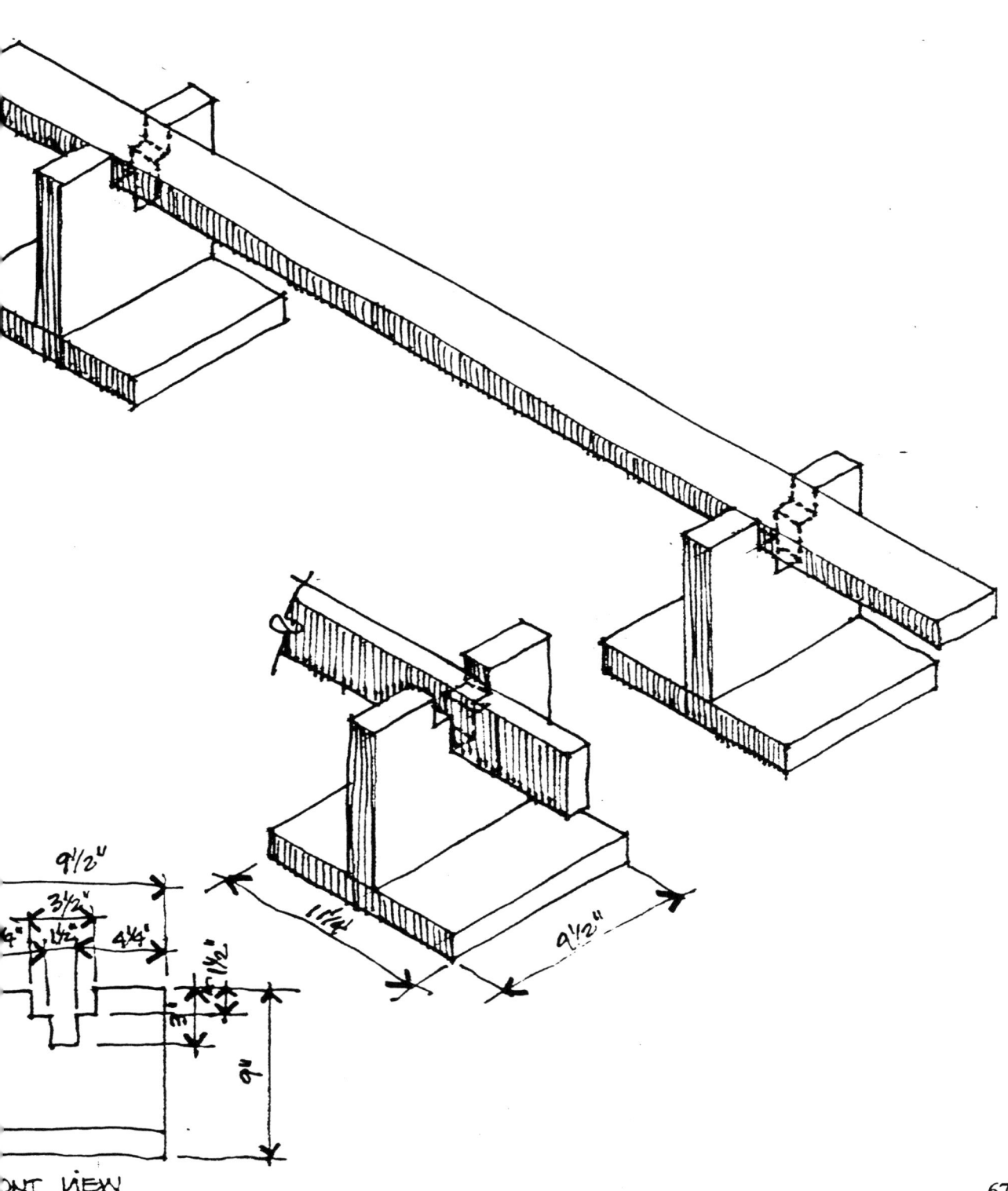

FRONT VIEW

Designing Effective Early Childhood Environments

## AREAS OF LEARNING

### Motor Skills

* Develops better stability and balance patterns in children.

* Spatial awareness becomes acute over time in knowing where the beam is and how the body needs to proportion itself over the beam to maintain balance. Distance to the floor is also learned.

* Eye-hand coordination is strengthened.

* Tactile-kinesthetic awareness is increased when the child uses all the senses during movement.

### Learning Skills

* Words or ideas such as balance, top, fall, under, next to, sideways, backwards, gymnast, tight-rope artist, over and across are all learned.

### Emotional Skills

* Concentration is required and challenges are presented for young children because it requires a different balancing technique, in addition to suspense and curiosity about the beam.

* The individual activity that a feeling of success when an act is accomplished.

### Social Skills

* Children learn to take turns on the beam and to respect others when they are on the beam at the same time.

* Put mats under the beam to become "water." Children become the "shark" or go in for a "swim" after jumping off the "bridge." Stories such as "The Three Billy Goats Gruff" can be played out on the beam.

### Suggestions

* The beam becomes a bridge, walk way or a tight rope.

* Music adds to the way the children use the beam.

* Young children should begin with tape on the floor and then a wider beam on the smaller steps. At first children may need to hold an adult's hand. They will tell you when they wish to try all alone. Then moving sideways, backwards, carrying something across, and with the beam on its side/edge to provide a smaller area on which to balance can be tried as they feel confident.

# Chapter 5: Suggested Equipment for Early Childhood Environments

* Primary grade children profit from this kind of practice in bodily awareness.

# Carpeted Blocks

Carpeted blocks are used as steps, individual play areas, seats, walks for a castle and house or placed side by side to form a stage. They are sturdy enough to stand on but can also be a table for doll dishes, manipulatives, writing or holding books.

The blocks are made with either one-half or three-fourths inch pieces of plywood, nailed or screwed together. Put a rope handle in place before the final assembly. Finally, tack and glue carpet pieces to all sides. Different sizes and lengths make the carpet blocks inviting.

## AREAS OF LEARNING

### Motor Skills

* Large muscle coordination is developed when the blocks are moved, dragged, pushed, turned over, jumped from, or used as steps.

* Dynamic balance is tested when children maintain their balance while moving the blocks.

* Children understand their position in space through the spatial properties of the blocks (size, form, position) in relation to themselves.

* Children explore spatial awareness when discovering how the blocks are similar or can be used alone or together.

* Combine two or three blocks for a different dimension or perspective of the environment.

### Language Skills

* Positional words are learned.

* Shape and texture features are discovered as in square, rectangle, flat, bumpy, rough, smooth, tough, squishy, spongy and colors.

* When sociodramatic props are included, social language occurs.

### Emotional Skills

* Carpet blocks are quiet areas for individual play or jumping, hiding and being with friends. Energy can be expended or a child can create a getaway place by adding pillows and blankets.

* Blocks are inviting and add variety with different colors, carpet textures and by being placed in different areas.

Designing Effective Early Childhood Environments

# CARPETED BLOCK

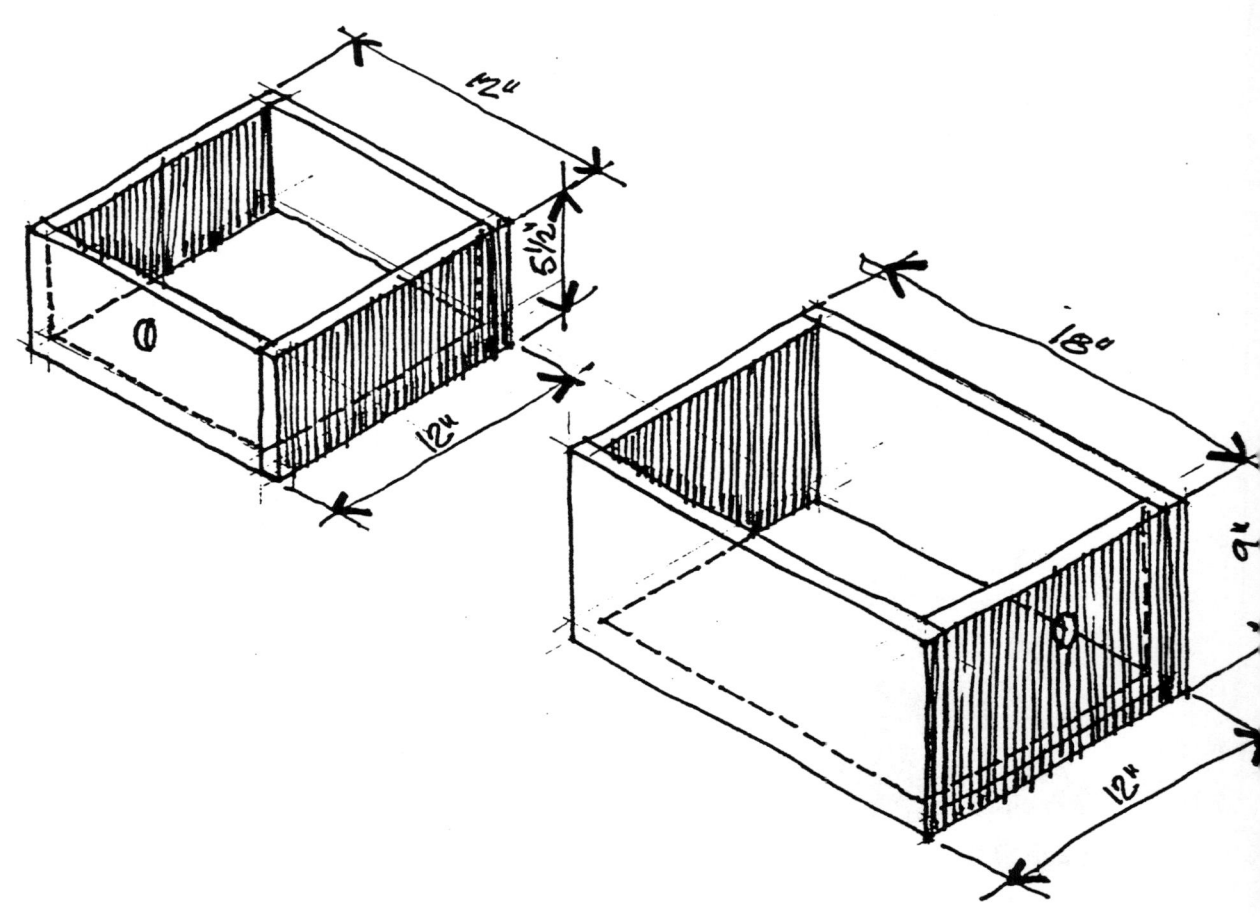

### Social Skills

* A hideaway built from joining two or three blocks can be a quiet conversational time for two or three children. They can watch the rest of the class or just stay in their private place.

* Add dress up clothes and the experience is more social.

* A quiet place for reading, investigating or writing in a journal can be created.

### Suggestion

* Just about any item can be added to carpet blocks to enhance learning.

# Gas Pump

The gas pump is easy to make out of a cardboard box and old garden hose or it can be made sturdier for longer use. It expands learning outdoors or in a classroom with indoor riding equipment. If a small overhang is built low on an outdoor wall of a building as a garage for the tricycles, the combination of gas pump and garages enhances sociodramatic play outside.

## AREAS OF LEARNING

### Motor Skills

* Eye-hand coordination increases.

* Gross motor skills increase with bikes.

* Correspondence occurs when the child matches a bike with the pump or another bicycle in a parking slot.

### Language Skills

* Vocabulary for this piece of equipment includes parking space, garage, gas, gas pump and hose.

### Emotional Skills

* Children have success when they learn to ride bicycles.

* Garages and gas pumps are a part of everyday life experience.

### Social Skills

* Children take turns on the bicycles and at the gas pump.

Designing Effective Early Childhood Environments

# GAS PUMP

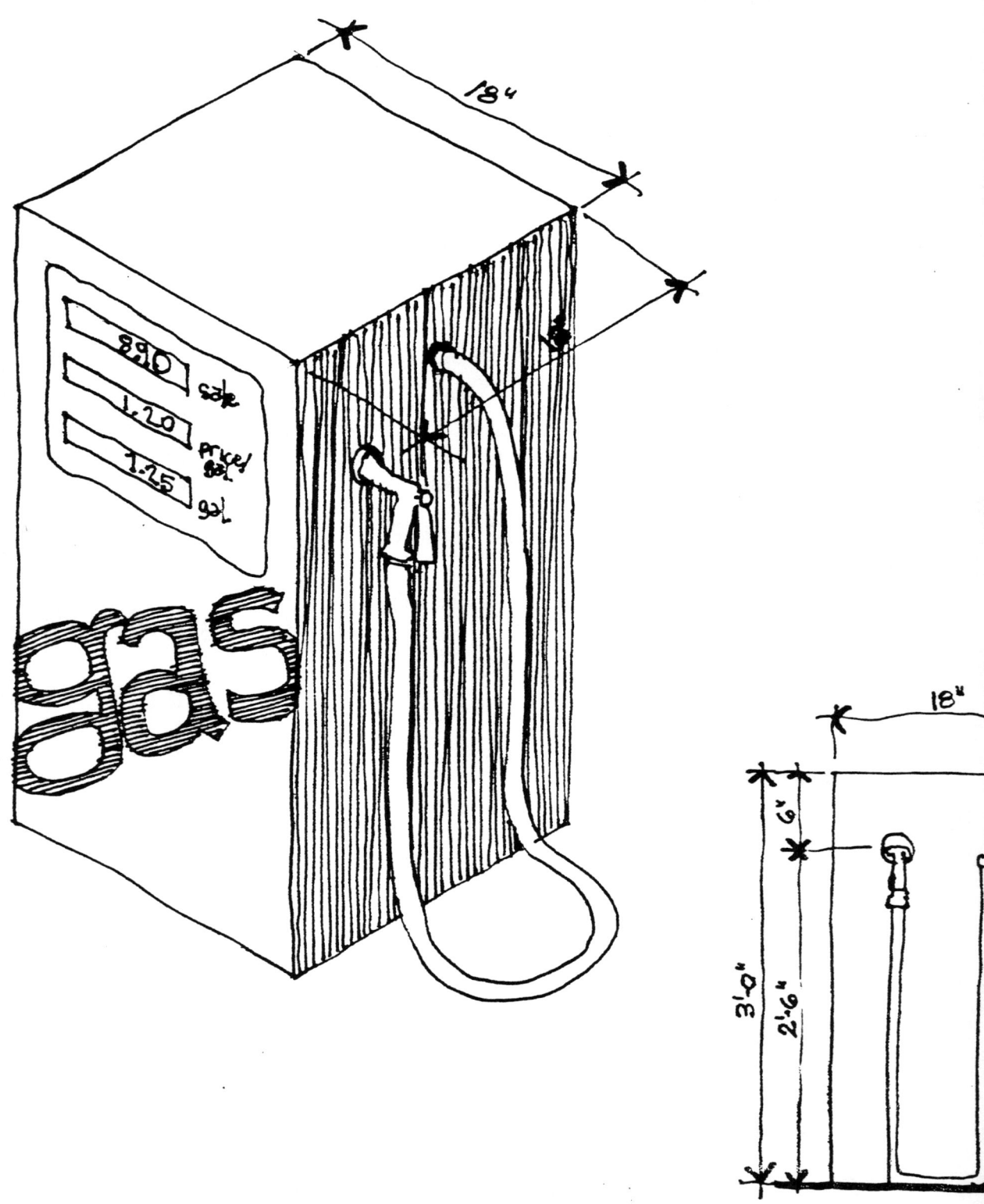

**Suggestions**

> * Add a cash register and play money to increase sociodramatic play.
> * Make signs for the roadways.

# Sand Box

There is so much to learn in a sandbox. In some areas of the country, children cannot get into sand during the cold months of the year. This indoor sand box allows for year-round learning and fun in the sand. This sandbox design defines the sand area and makes it inviting by being on different levels. It allows for different kinds of exploration in the sand, as compared to a combination water and sand table. The surfaces need to be smooth (possibly formica) for easy cleanup.

Construct this structure with 2"x12" boards as the frame and three-fourths inch plywood for the tops and sides. The plywood should have a very durable finish. Oil-based enamel is more difficult to apply, but is more durable than water-based paints.

**AREAS OF LEARNING**

**Motor Skills**

> * Eye-hand coordination is developed.
> * Understanding of top, back, front, and sides of a structure forming a three-dimensional object.
> * Learn about volume by digging holes and filling them with other materials and water.
> * Directions are learned when roads are made and cars driven along these roads.

**Language Skills**

> * Vocabulary about tools, cars, structures, and their components increases.
> * Social language occurs as children play next to one another.
> * Imaginations develop.

**Emotional Skills**

> * Sand is soothing, expressive and creative.
> * Children have control over how sand is used.

**Social Skills**

> * Children learn to share tools, cars and buckets.
> * Children cooperate in the construction of houses and roads.

# SAND BOX

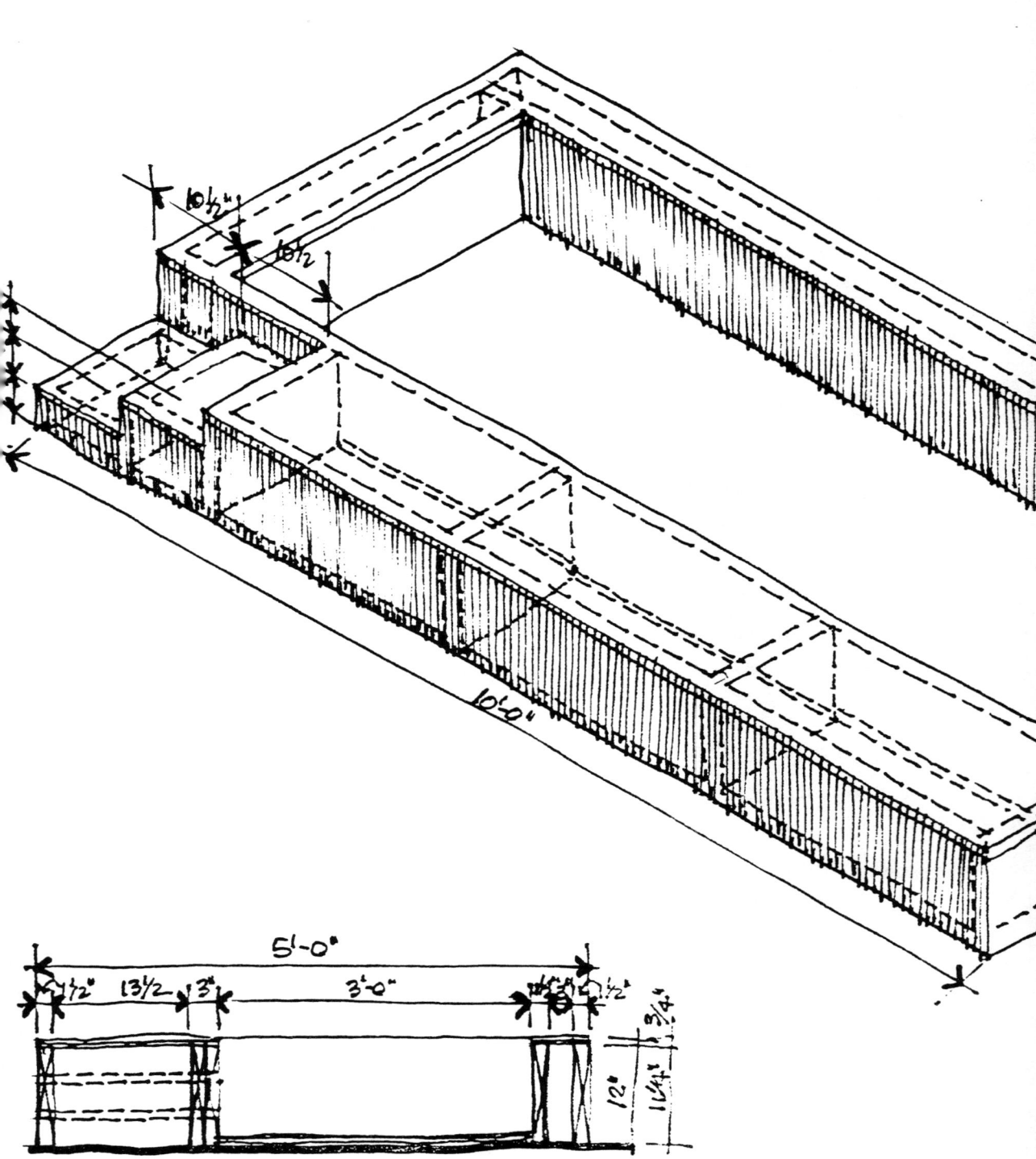

**Suggestion**

* Rotate different tools in the sandbox.

# Room Divider/Bulletin Board

The room divider/bulletin board is a piece of equipment that assists children to define space.

The room divider is made of 1"x 2" boards with quarter round pieces to finish it and help hold the homosote board in place. Burlap, wallpaper or felt can provide different surfaces. 1"x 6" boards are used for end supports.

**AREAS OF LEARNING**

**Motor Skills**

* Helps children understand traffic patterns in the classroom.
* Redirects children from open spaces to activity centers.

**Language Skills**

* Displays pictures and print pertaining to the theme or unit under study.
* Displays the names of the children.
* Flannel pieces teach about shapes, numbers and textures.

**Emotional Skills**

* Provides low space for children to display art papers or drawings.
* Provides a secluded place for two or three children.

**Social Skills**

* Provides a stage for a puppet theater and other drama productions.

**Suggestion**

* Easily moved to create a large area for music or creative movement.

# Side-by-Side Easels

Easel use is often a solitary endeavor but can facilitate social interaction if the easels are placed side by side. Young children who are often in the egocentric stage

# ROOM DIVIDER / BULLETIN BOARD

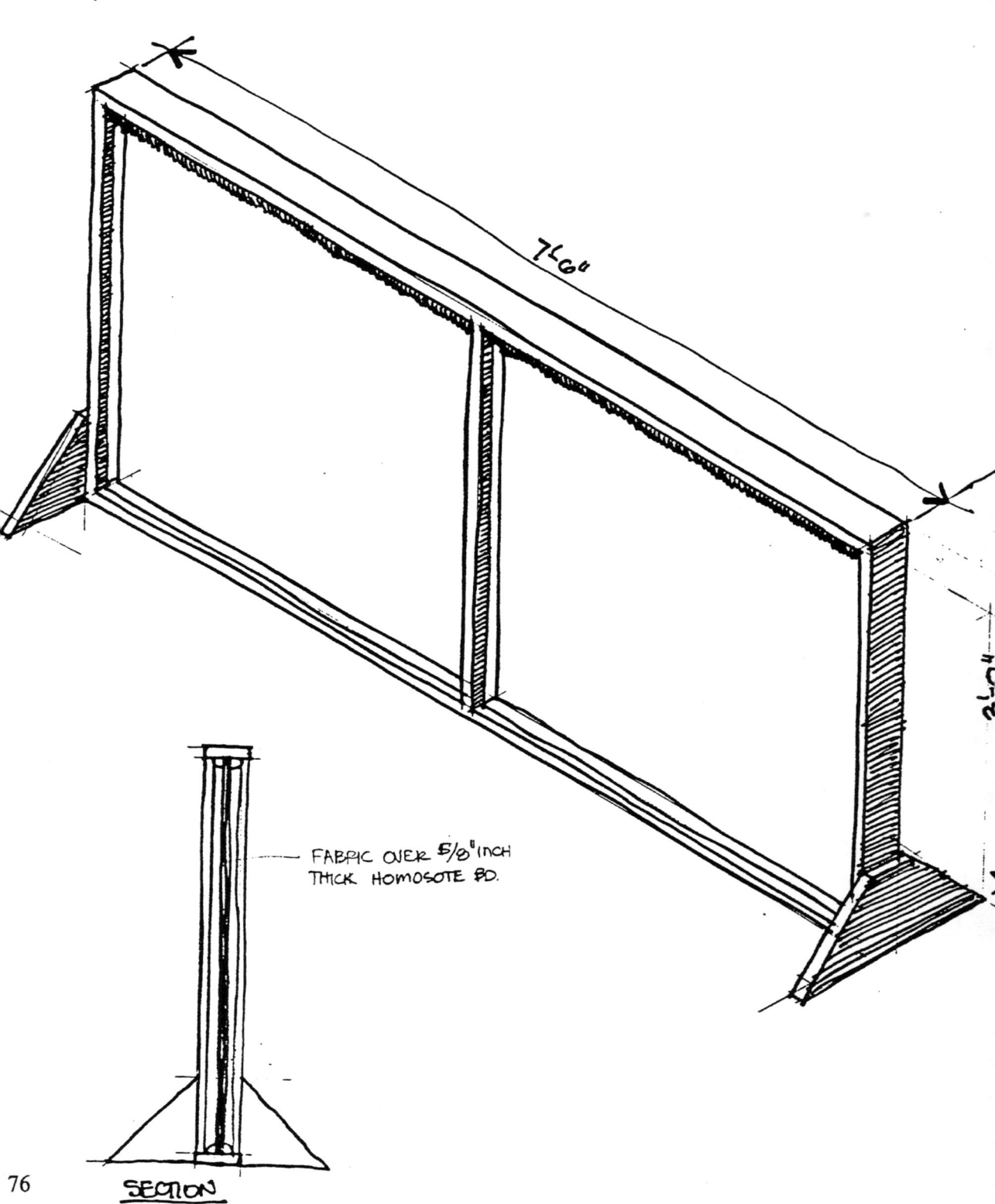

FABRIC OVER 5/8" INCH THICK HOMOSOTE BD.

SECTION

of development, may not be aware of others next to them, but once they have explored the materials and use them, they become more social and conversant while participating in the activity. Older children are curious about others and include others in their activities by watching and talking. This side-by-side arrangement brings the children together for peer interaction instead of teacher-child interaction.

These easels can be mounted on a wall or designed as free standing easels with two sides.

## AREAS OF LEARNING

**Motor Skills**

* Eye-hand coordination is enhanced.
* Visual perception increases as the child watches the movement of the brush.
* Balance is developed while doing a non-locomotor task.
* Form perception is developed when lines, curves and dots add up to a finished picture, showing that parts comprise a whole.

**Language Skills**

* Vocabulary increases according to lines, shapes, colors, labels of pictures and discussions with partners.
* Primary age children can add commentary, labels and sentences to their printings to enhance and extend concept development.

**Emotional Skills**

* Art is expressive and materials are explored more readily if the teacher does not interfere. Children should be free to create "just a picture" if they wish.
* Art is inviting because it can turn out differently every time.

**Social Skills**

* Children can watch each other and take turns painting, labeling and communicating.

**Suggestions**

* Use two brushes taped together in a "V" formation.
* Use one color--but various shades of that color.

Designing Effective Early Childhood Environments

## SIDE BY SIDE EASLES

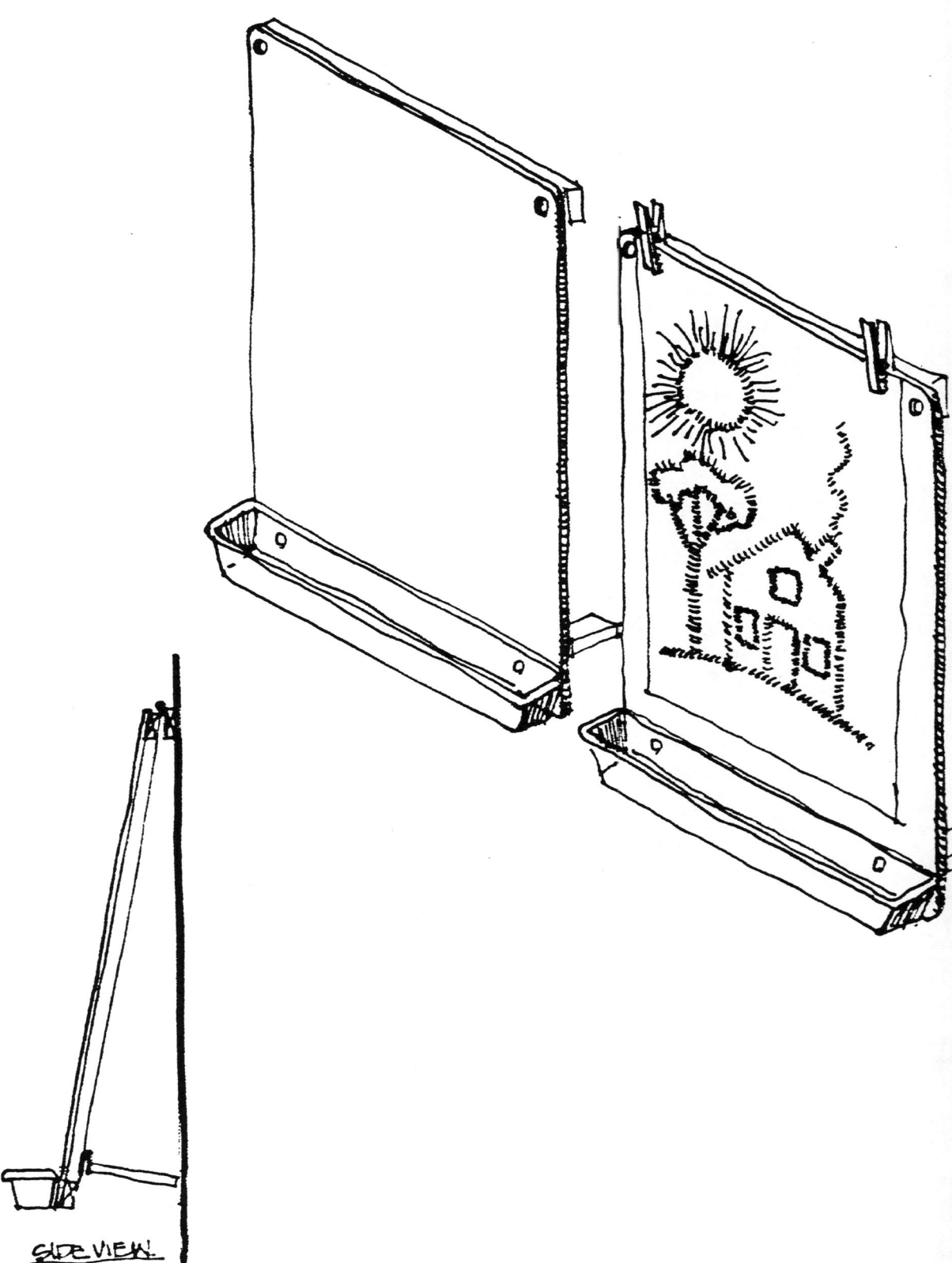

SIDE VIEW

* Try helmet painting where a brush is attached to a football helmet and the child uses the head instead of hand.

* Try little brushes or little rollers or sponges held with clothespins.

* Use a broomstick handle with the brush attached to the end. Lots of room will be needed!

# Telephone Booth

The telephone booth is an excellent addition to an early childhood classroom. Three, four and five year olds can practice social language on the telephone. The children need to stay near the phone when using the instrument. The booth should be attached to the wall or other sturdy structure to avoid having the booth topple over. Adding 2"x6" boards around the base of the booth will help to keep it from toppling over. The frame of the booth is constructed of 2"x2" boards with 1/4" plywood semi-enclosing the frame. Use an old, real telephone in the booth.

**Areas of Learning**

**Motor Skills**

* Eye-hand coordination is strengthened.

* Static balance increases while maintaining balance when dialing and "conversing."

* Encoding occurs when the child expresses ideas and thoughts through speech, posture or body movements when "on the phone."

* Sequential memory is tested when reproducing a set of events or actions from memory. An example is repeating a phone call to grandmother. The conversation may go like this: "When are you coming to visit? Remember to bring your suit. When are you going to get here? Daddy will pick you up. See you for dinner. Bye."

**Language Skills**

* Many communication skills are explored.

* Reaffirming and reassuring talk takes place.

* Time-related vocabulary include, before, after, tonight, tomorrow, soon and later.

Designing Effective Early Childhood Environments

## TELEPHONE BOOTH

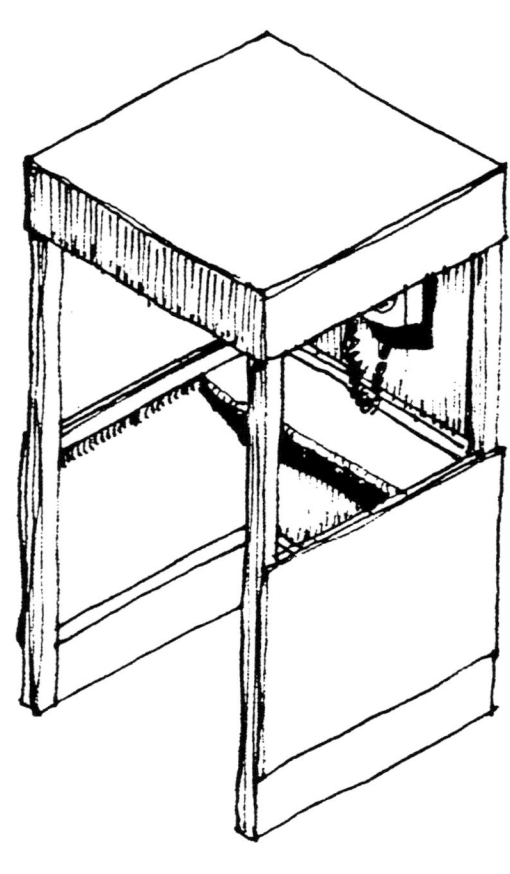

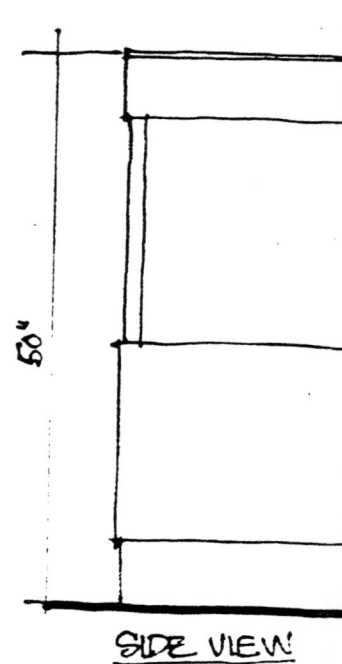

SIDE VIEW

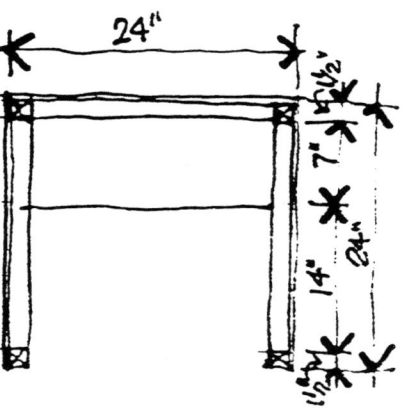

PLAN VIEW

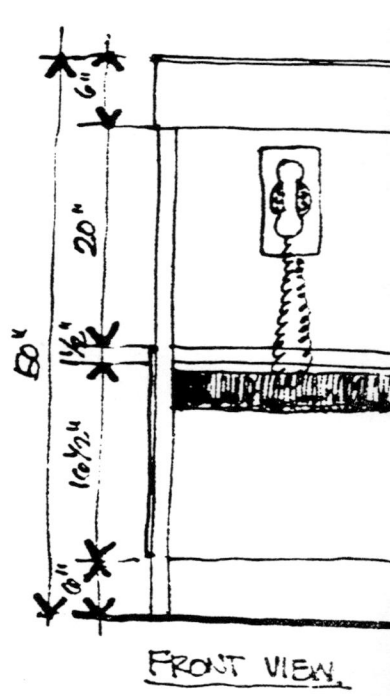

FRONT VIEW

## Emotional Skills

* A telephone is helpful for children who miss being at home. The "call" home to find out what is going on and when they will go home is often comforting.

* Children see the telephone everyday, so it is part of their everyday experience.

* A telephone is always inviting.

## Social Skills

* The telephone is used individually but children connect conversations on the phone to someone close by.

## Suggestions

* The telephone is used in the housekeeping area or other sociodramatic areas to extend phone calls to a doctor, mother, father, friend or a store.

# Salt Swing

This salt swing comes from an idea in George E. Foreman's and Fleet Hill's book Constructive Play: Applying Piaget in Preschool. (1980) Salt (or other material) freely falling from the funnel is inviting and a wonder to young children. Younger children will just enjoy watching the salt fall and the funnel swing. Other children will position the funnel first and try different positions to make their "designs." Younger, more egocentric children think their push is the only thing that makes the funnel go. Older children begin to understand that their push begins the process but the weight inside will continue the back and forth motion until gravity pulls it to the center. This structure resembles a small saw horse made out of 2"x4" boards. The funnel can be plastic or a paper paint strainer with the tip cut off. The funnel is attached to the cross beam with string.

## AREAS OF LEARNING

## Motor Skills

* Young children cannot trace moving objects, but the swing helps to develop ocular and visual pursuits by "freezing" the movement--trails left by the sand/salt.

* Children are concerned with what happens with things. The salt trails show the pattern the swing takes.

* Force and weight properties (gravity) are explored. When the swing is pushed, it always comes back and stops in the middle.

## SALT SWING

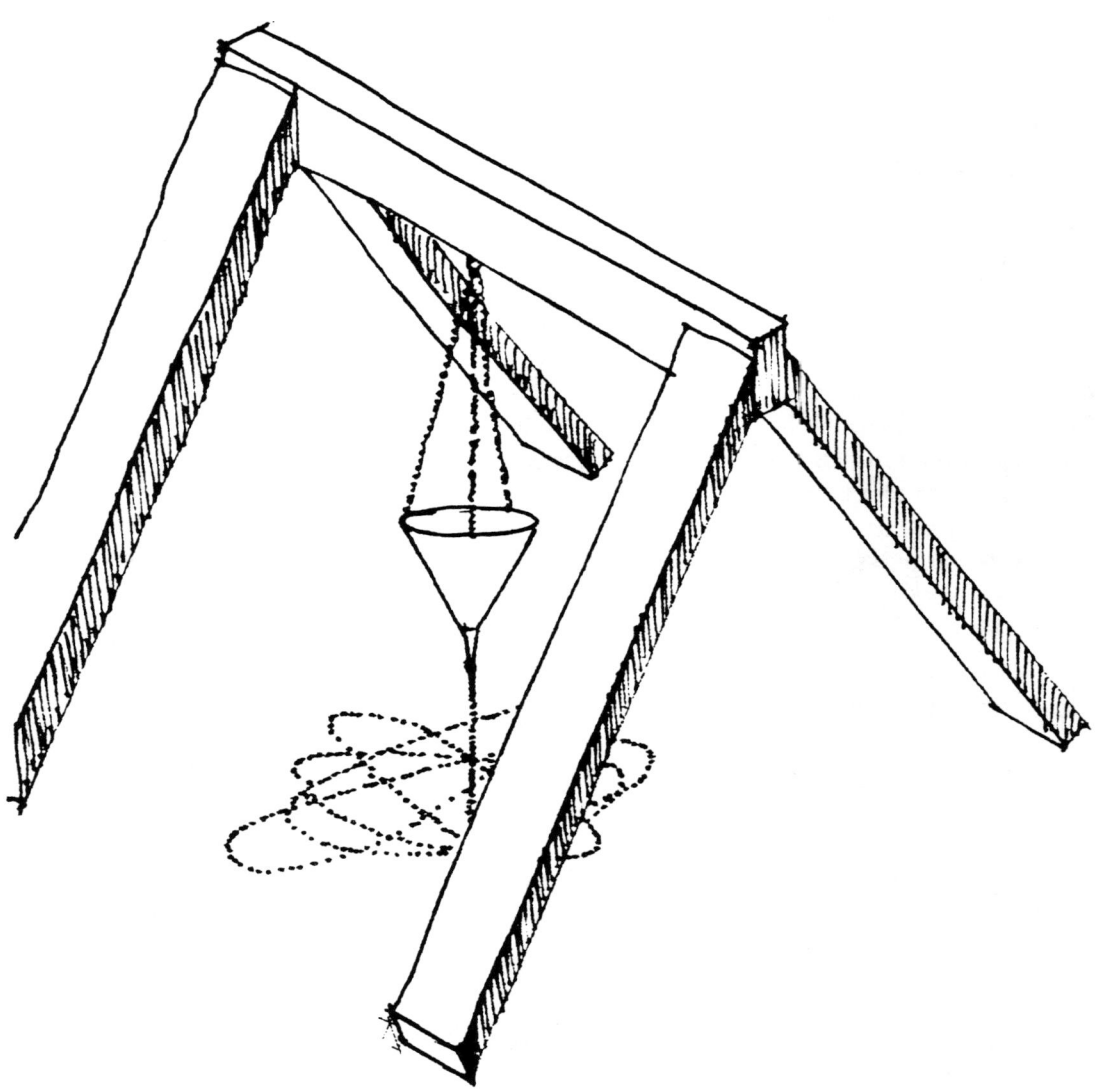

* Vacant areas are identified where the funnel did not go.
* Eye-hand coordination is strengthened.

**Language Skills**

* New vocabulary is learned, such as: swing, drop, patterns, trails, hanging heavy/light, thick/thin, smooth/rough.

**Emotional Skills**

* Free motion is soothing.
* There is a feeling of success in putting something in motion.

**Social Skills**

* Children learn to take turns pushing the swing.

**Suggestions**

* To save a design, school glue can be "painted" on the paper and then the salt can drop onto this.
* For colored salt, the children can help stir soft colored chalk into bowls of white salt.
* If using paint or glue in the funnel, play around with the consistency of the paint and periodically watch for clogging of the glue.
* A plastic ketchup bottle filled with sand suspended from the ceiling will create wonderful designs and tracks on white or dark paper covering the floor.
* A tennis ball or racquetball attached to the swinging string knocks down pins or blocks.

# Clear Writing Easel

Most programs have an easel or two. Primarily used for painting or chalk drawing, they also can be a good visual aid for group time. This easel is easily stored behind a door or any other out-of-the-way spot. It is easy to keep clean and inviting because it is different in its appearance from most easels. The easel is used as the language experience easel and is explained with an example under "Language Skills" below.

The easel is made with 1"x 2" boards, screws, one hinge, linked chain and plexiglass.

## CLEAR WRITING EASLE

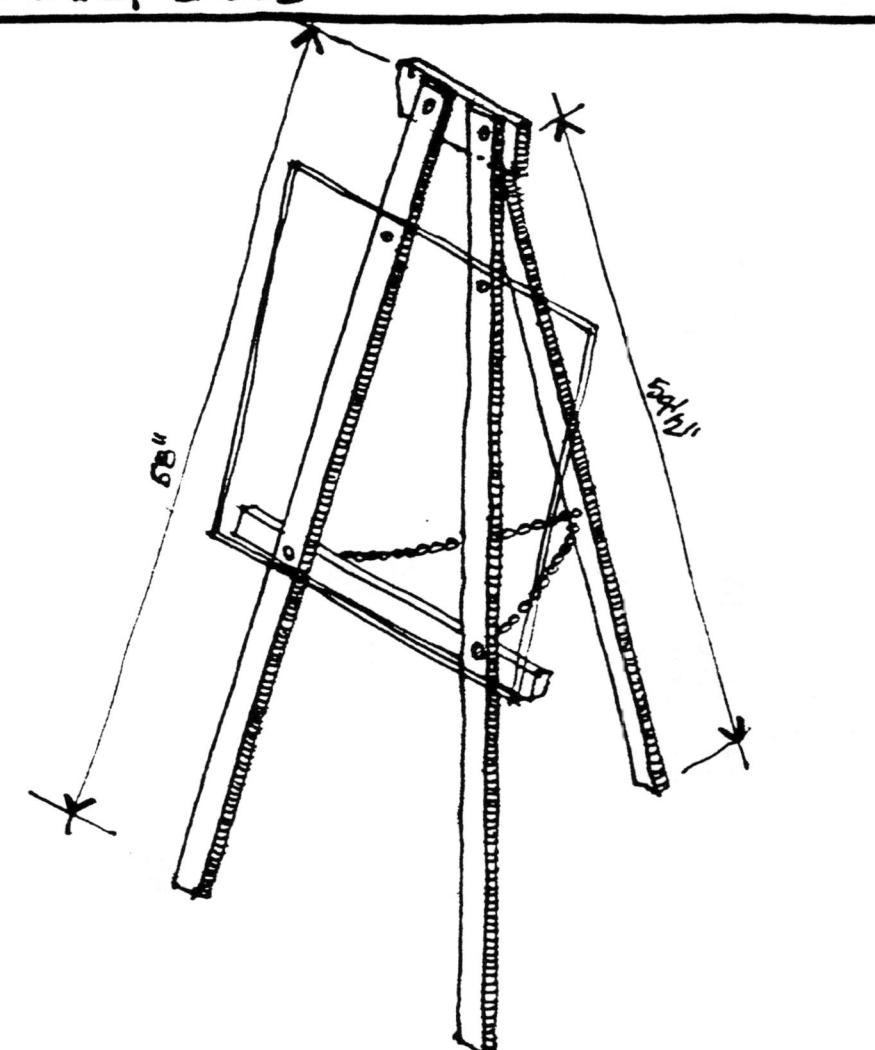

# Chapter 5: Suggested Equipment for Early Childhood Environments

## AREAS OF LEARNING

### Motor Skills

* A different perspective on writing and additional arm movement is gained when writing/drawing at the easel.

* Figure ground is enhanced with the clear back that allows for focusing on the content.

* Some decoding of written words will occur.

### Language Skills

* Language experience charts are a gathering tool for all the vocabulary that go with a theme. Example: The teacher writes the words that go with the theme selected by the children. A sample theme is "pets." Resulting vocabulary include dog, cat, hamster, turtle, toad, Guinea pig, gerbil, fish, bird, ants, kitten, puppy, and rock.

* Data gathered during the unit is recorded by the teacher as the children dictate.

* Charts completed can be placed in the environment for reference.

* Stories written by the group can be recorded.

* Sharing items brought to the classroom can be recorded.

* Any information the teacher wishes to tell the children can be read from this chart.

* Directions are shared and available.

* A model for printing, spelling, and concepts can be in front of the children at all times.

### Emotional Skills

* Self-esteem is developed when the child's contribution is valued by being recorded.

* Success in a group experience also is important.

### Social Skills

* Children take turns when giving suggestions.

* Two children can draw at the easel at the same time and develop sharing behaviors.

### Suggestions

* Children draw on the easel with a variety of writing utensils.

* Plexiglass front can be used with markers and a damp cloth as the eraser.

# Felt/Flannel Easel

The flannel board is another tool for storytelling. The one designed here has two sides on which two children can play with flannel board shapes or figures. As with the writing easel, language is enhanced through telling, labeling, counting, matching and sharing.

The legs of this easel are made with 1"x3" boards with hinges at the top. Linked chain keeps the legs from slipping out too far. One-half inch plywood provides for the two flannel board bases. These can be screwed or nailed in place. Flannel is then glued to the plywood to provide a surface on which felt shapes and characters will adhere. A tray at the base of the easel is useful, but optional.

## AREAS OF LEARNING

### Motor Skills

* Fine motor control is strengthened.
* Figure ground is developed as children chose the felt figures.
* Form perception develops when fitting pieces together to create a design.
* Sorting and classifying occurs with shape, color and number cut-outs.

### Language Skills

* Names of shapes and colors are learned. Texture words such as soft, rough, smooth or bumpy are used. Attributes include striped, plain, dotted and spotted can be discussed.
* Stories are retold and re-enacted on a flannel board.
* Math and counting concepts are practiced, and vocabulary (more, less, bigger, smaller, little, big, some, taller, longer, shorter and numbers) is used.

### Emotional Skills

* Imaginative and creative fears and hopes are played out in a non-threatening way.
* The easel allows for individual exploration.

### Social Skills

* Children take turns re-enacting a story or telling the story together, each taking different roles.
* Negotiation skills are practiced when children decide who will do what task or how many pieces of felt they will use.

## Chapter 5: Suggested Equipment for Early Childhood Environments

# FELT/FLANNEL EASEL

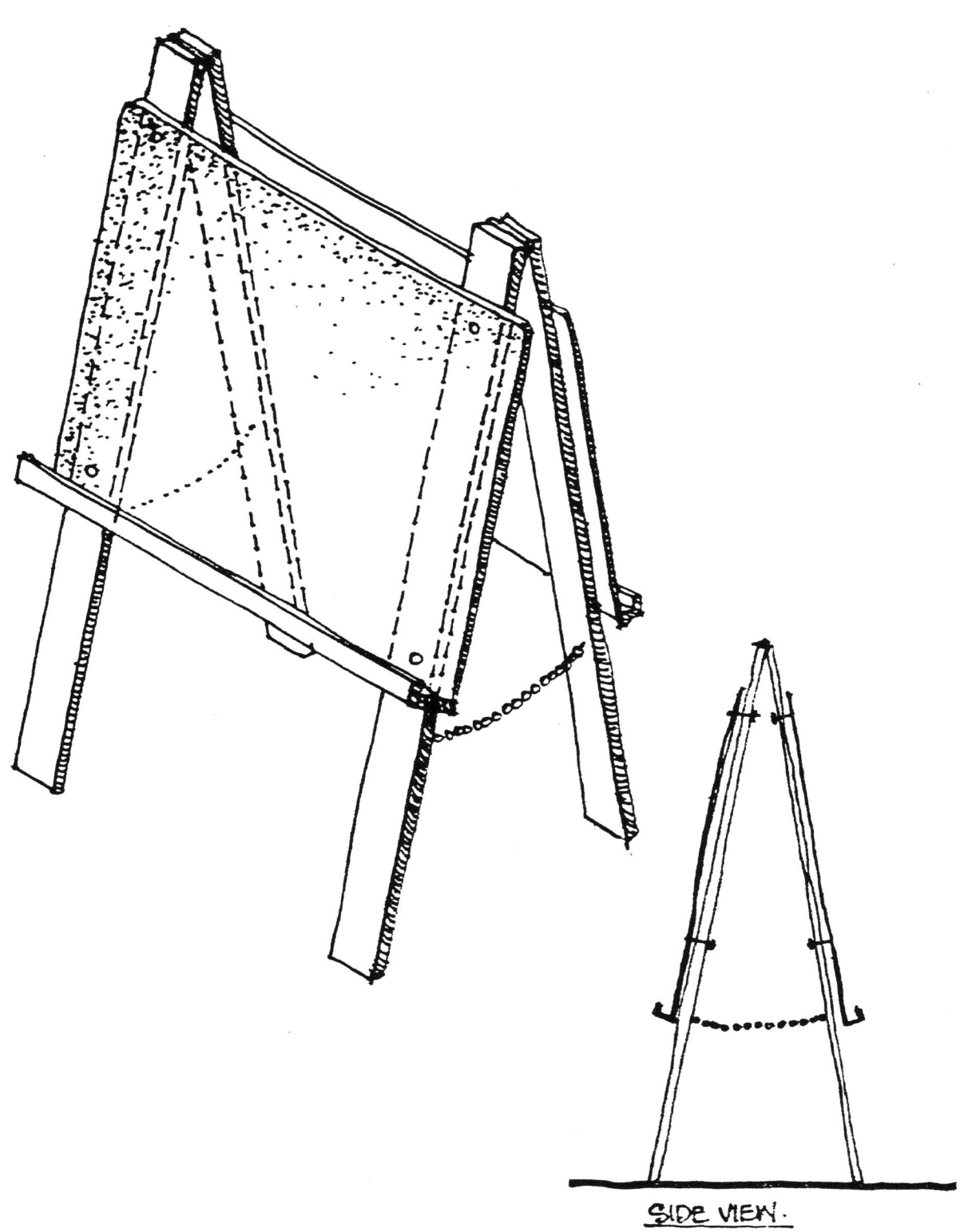

SIDE VIEW.

## Suggestion

* Flannel board pieces can be numbers, letters, designs, or based on stories and nursery rhymes.

# Bean Bag Toss

The bean bag toss is a lot of fun and a noncompetitive activity for young children. They explore distance and want to know where the bean bag lands. Older children, on the otherhand, understand the force and accuracy needed and make a competitive game out of it.

Bean bag toss structures are made out of boxes or a piece of 1/2" plywood with a painted finish. Shapes are cut into the front with 1"x 3" boards hinged on the back to support the board at a slight angle. String or chain can keep the support boards from slipping away.

## AREAS OF LEARNING

### Motor Skills

* Children understand force through both throwing and receiving the bean bag.
* Estimation of the distance thrown is learned.
* Eye-hand coordination is developed.
* Weight and balance is explored when the bag is on top of the head or shoulder.
* Tactile-kinesthetic awareness is strengthened through manipulation of the bean bag.

### Language Skills

* Descriptive vocabulary for movement and placement such as up, down, over, through, throw, toss, into, on, under, behind, next to and beside.
* Children learn to label identified shapes.

## Chapter 5: Suggested Equipment for Early Childhood Environments

**Emotional Skills**

* Serves as an outlet for stress or tension.

* Explore-uses of the body and strengths include throwing, catching, balancing with different parts of the body, shaking, or slapping against the opposite hand, or knees.

**Social Skills**

* Taking turns and keeping track of the number of throws that go through the holes.

* Cooperation is learned when throwing and catching becomes a joint effort.

**Suggestions**

* Bean bags of different sizes, shapes and colors can be made.

* Soft, spongy balls and racquetballs are fun to use for variety.

# BEAN BAG TOSS

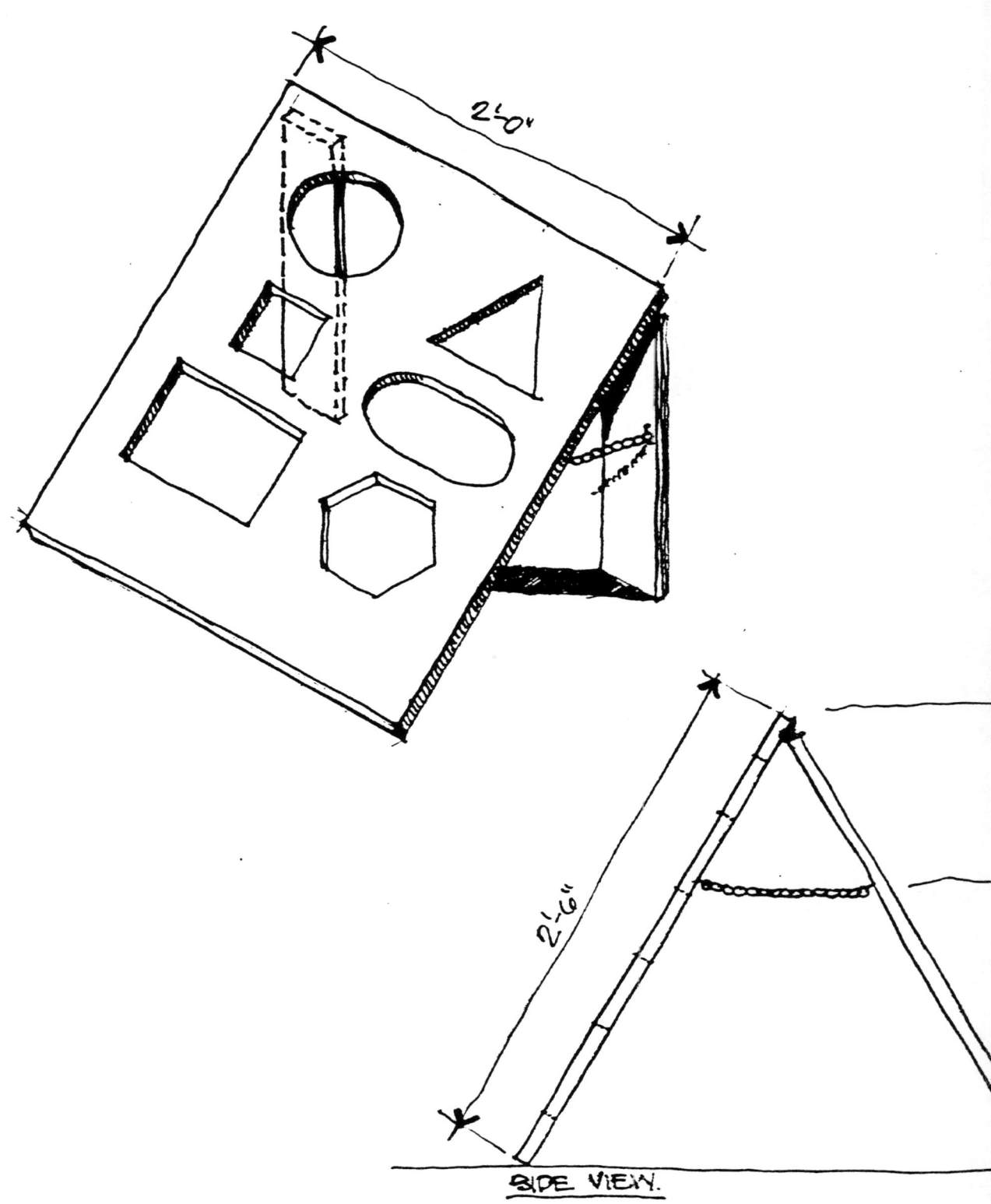

SIDE VIEW.

# Smock Holder/Dress Up Clothes Tree

This "tree" is used for many different things: smocks dry on it, clothes hang on it, or purses and hats hang from it. This provides a place where children return items at clean up time. It is constructed from a 4"x 4" post with holes for pegs drilled at an angle. The pegs are dowels, one inch in diameter and approximately five to six inches long. The base is created from 1"x 6" boards, one foot long. These can be nailed or screwed into the 4"X 4" post.

## AREAS OF LEARNING

### Motor Skills

* Eye-hand coordination is developed when replacing a purse, shirt or smock.
* Static balance is used when an item is returned.
* Distance is explored when hanging up a smock on offset pegs.

### Language Skills

* Explore these words: pegs, tree, smocks, dress up items, aprons and hang up.

### Emotional Skills

* Success is achieved when retrieving and returning articles.

### Social Skill

* The "tree" provides an easy way to visually tell children when articles are being used. Children realize if they return an article, someone else then uses it...and it will be there when they want to use it another time.

### Suggestion

* This "tree" can be placed in many areas including housekeeping, art, storage and the teacher's area.

# SMOCK HOLDER / DRESS UP CLOTHESTREE

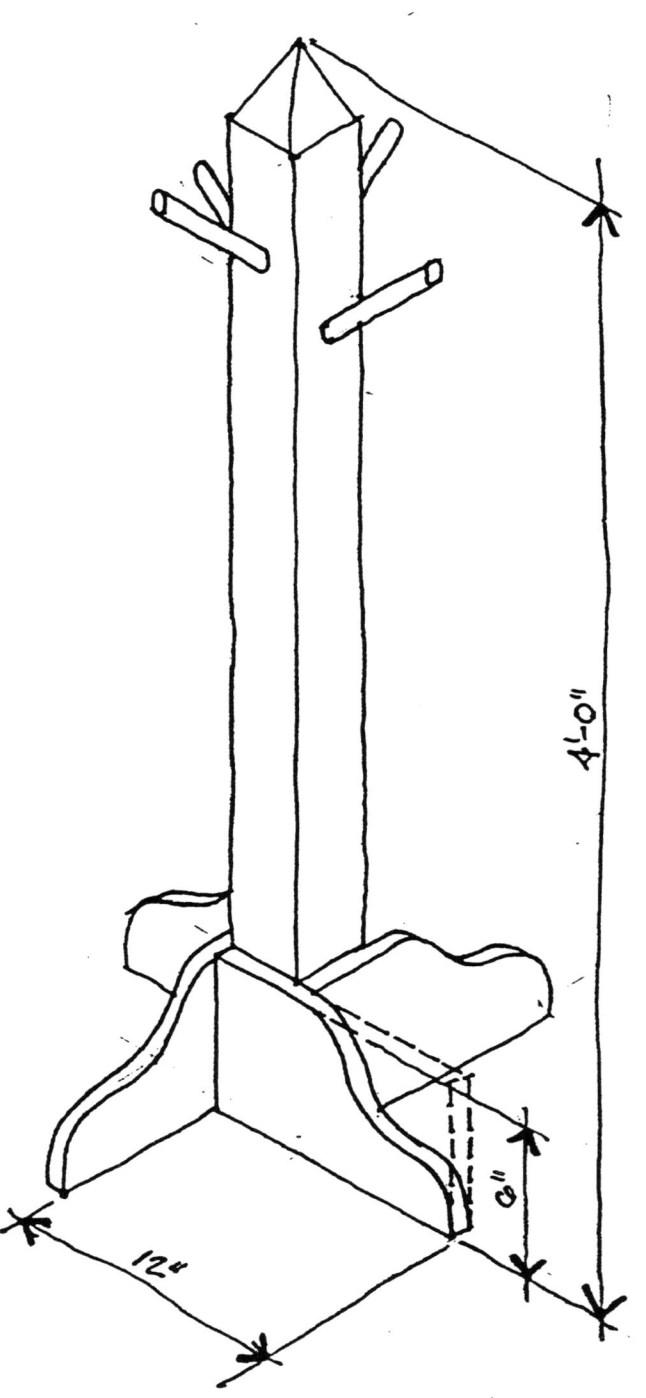

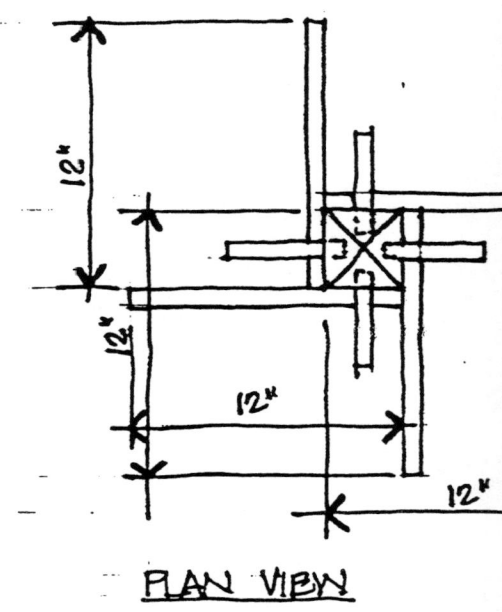

PLAN VIEW

Chapter 5: Suggested Equipment for Early Childhood Environments

# Loft

A loft is ideal for a sociodramatic area because it defines space for play and the area around it. This structure is too heavy to move around the room so it is an area that needs to change from within. Suggestions for these changes are listed at the end of this section.

Changes enhance and capitalize on children's skills, growth and interests. (Loughlin and Suina, 1982) There are many everyday experiences a child observes and clarifies through dramatic play and the experiences and emotions that go with them. Dramatic play allows children to express their inner needs. Dramatics present experiences that offer great opportunities for learning to cope with others. (Butler et al., 1978) Interaction with peers grows over time. Repeat the same dramatic play area themes later in the year to watch how the children have matured. This repetition will allow children to try different roles they may not have explored the first time.

The loft needs to be sturdy. The durable framework is built from 4"x 4" posts with 2"x 4" boards. The floors are 3/4" pieces of plywood that rest on a 2"x 4" frame. Holes are drilled through the top parts of the 4"x 4" posts, through which to string the rope. To achieve a more finished look, 1"x 4" boards can be placed around the outside of the floor frames. The structure must be built inside the classroom, because it will not fit through a standard door frame. Check with local authorities to determine whether two levels are permissible in the school.

## AREAS OF LEARNING

### Motor Skills

* A loft defines space and children learn boundaries.

* Steps on the ladder develop visual figure ground perception.

* Steps on the ladder develop balancing abilities.

* Steps on the ladder develop locomotor patterns in eye-foot coordination.

* Steps on the ladder develop *homolateral* movement (moving the limbs on one side of the body in unison).

* Depending on the contents in the loft, eye-hand coordination can be enhanced. Children develop *kinesthetically* (knowing how to move the body by recalling previous experiences.

* The "upstairs," or the top of the loft, can be used for relaxing the muscles and gives a different visual perspective.

### Language Skills

* Dramatic play gives opportunities for learning new vocabulary, social skills and communication skills.

* Props are labeled and remembered.

**Emotional Skills**

* Dramatics offer a way to express creativity in characters and use of materials or props.

* Young children expand their experiences through dramatic play.

**Suggestions**

* Check local ordinances and with inspectors to see if two levels are permitted in a classroom. If two levels are not allowed, then the structure can be a canopy-type unit or resemble more of a house.

* Add posters, props, colors and textures to the area.

* Minimize confusion by providing hooks for clothes and other articles, and glue shapes on the shelves for organized storage of items.

* Have enough materials--but be careful not to have too much.

**Loft Themes**

The size of the area determines the number of children in the area which determines the amount of materials that are appropriate.

* The loft can house a library, complete with shelves, books, stamps and ink pads, a typewriter, and posters. Tables, chairs, cushions and pillows can be added for reading comfort.

* To create a restaurant, menus can be constructed by placing pictures of food on laminated paper, providing note pads for orders, chef hats, aprons, a stove, plates, cups, a cash register with play money, table and chairs (these could be placed outside the loft) -- even a restaurant sign.

* A pizza parlor stems from the same concept with round pieces of cardboard for pizza pans, white felt circles for crust, red felt circles for tomato sauce, felt shapes cut into mushrooms, pepperoni, peppers, onions and cheese

* To create a spaceship, enclose the loft with butcher paper, complete with a door cut out. An American flag and "U.S.A." can be painted on the outside paper and steering wheels drawn inside. Spacesuits are made out of foil and headphones, helmets, chairs, computers or typewriters, and a small table for exploration of rocks and sand with magnifying glasses will complete the galactic setting.

* A sporting goods store will come to life with old skis, helmets, baseball hats, swimming gear, balls and a cash register.

* Take a field trip to a cider mill to encourage the construction of a similated mill. Gallon jugs and blocks for a "press," to set the stage.

# Chapter 5: Suggested Equipment for Early Childhood Environments

LOFT

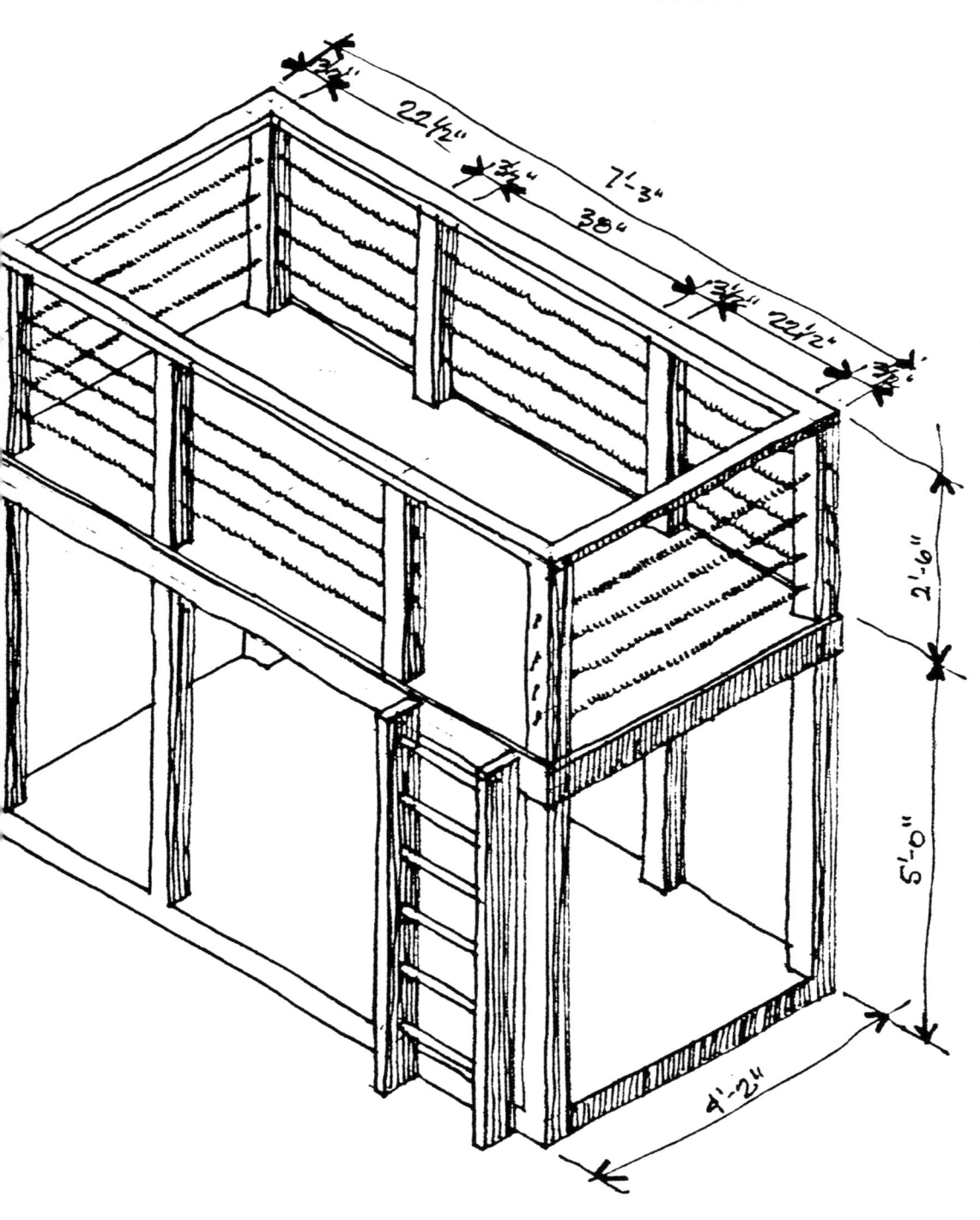

## Designing Effective Early Childhood Environments

* Pet Store/Veterinarian Hospital-- Stuffed animals, animal dishes, cash register with play money, paper and pencils for "lists," boxes made into cages, lab coats and gloves.

* Camping-- Tent, benches, Coleman stove (old one, donated)pans, cups, mugs, silverware, walking sticks, blow up raft, fishing gear (no hooks), some games or cards, lanterns or flashlights and sleeping bags.

* Mechanics Shop-- Riding toys, gas pumps, cash register with play money, computer, tools to tighten nuts, old parts of cars or nuts, bolts, steering wheels, old car radio, knobs, screws, boards and screwdrivers.

* Castle-- Crowns, hats, gowns, jewelry, chairs, castle front made out of boxes, flags, hat boxes and containers.

* House-- Stove, sink, refrigerator, table, chairs, dishes and place settings, dress up clothes, including shoes, purses, briefcases, hats, gloves, scarves and jewelry.

* Grocery Store-- Shelves for old cartons of milk, cereal, crackers and other food items, cash register with play money, shopping carts, if available (child size) and bags.

# Car

This unit was constructed by four different people in a child care center. It is an excellent example of a collaborative effort to produce a product. Donations, such as steering wheels from a junkyard, paint and a plumbing outlet for piping add extra touches. This unit can be placed anywhere and is easily moved to different classrooms. Children practice their everyday experiences.

Use 2"x 4" boards, plywood and 3/4" pipe for the car. The pipe should have threads to secure a pipe knob to the end. The steering wheel is held in place by the pipe knob. Portable radios are optional.

### AREAS OF LEARNING

**Motor Skills**

* Eye-hand coordination.

* Development of sequential memory as children get in, buckle up, lock door, turn key, steer, call police, announce the destination, turn off key, unbuckle, open door and get out.

**Language Skills**

* Vocabulary learned includes far, long, over, turn, stop, go, drive, fast, slow, up, down, bump, engine, tires, fix, open, close, out, in, trunk, hood, pedals, steering wheel and gauges.

Chapter 5: Suggested Equipment for Early Childhood Environments

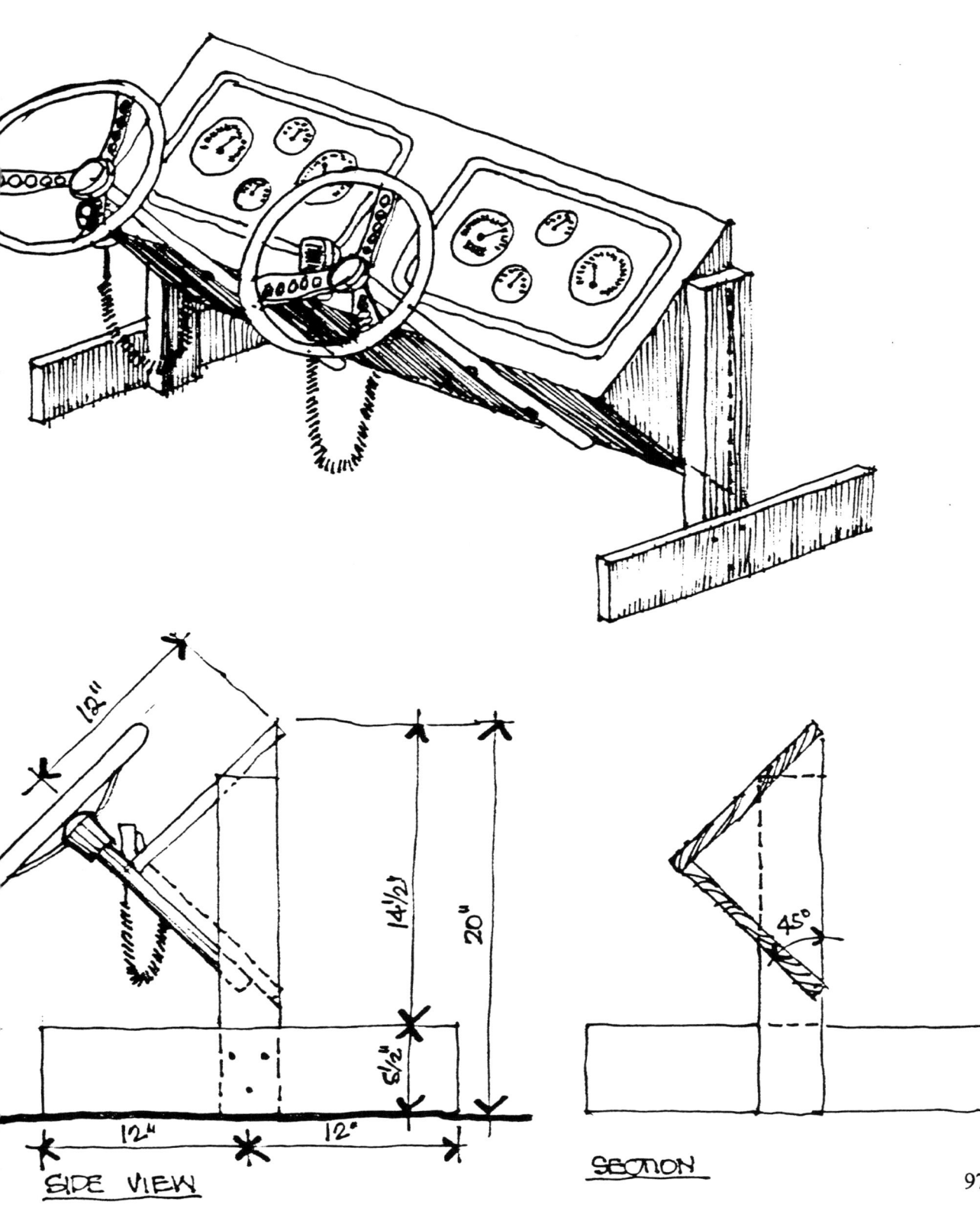

SIDE VIEW

SECTION

## Emotional Skills

* Children practice everyday skills.
* Children gain a sense of accomplishment when they reach the "destination."
* The car encourages imagination.

## Social Skills

* Children take turns steering and talking to each other on the Citizens Band Radios.
* "Drivers" give directions to passengers.
* Cooperation is needed in travel.

## Suggestions

* Add blocks for pedals.
* Add suitcases or dress up clothes.
* Place the unit in the sociodramatic area when it is a space ship or an airplane.
* Place the unit in front of a mirror.

Chapter 5: Suggested Equipment for Early Childhood Environments

# Room Arrangements for Preschools and Kindergartens

The following room and corner arrangements are suggested to individualize preschool and kindergarten programs so children do not need constant teacher supervision. The arrangements enable the teacher to have immediate visibility of every part of the room.

These room arrangements illustrate how equipment is implemented in the classroom. Corners of this arrangement show one, two or three areas combined. These enable teachers to work on a specific area and change the whole room.

Arrows indicate the flow of traffic. Windows are not marked, but need to be considered. These arrangements include multi-level structures, but prior to any construction, secure approval from the state department of social services or other local licensing agencies.

**Figure 1** shows a large room with many of the suggested structures. This arrangement has noisy/quiet and wet/dry areas. The upper left quarter of the room is the quiet/wet area containing the water and science tables and sink. The upper right quarter is the noisy/wet area with the sand box. The lower left is the quiet/dry section with books, puzzles, writing tables and cozy areas. The lower right section is the noisy/dry area with the loft, dress up clothes, blocks and manipulatives.

Carpeted blocks are in two different areas for different purposes. They create individual work spaces next to the puzzles, and next to the blocks used for construction. The room divider near the top of the classroom helps direct traffic into the different areas. This room is narrow and the angles assist in defining the interest areas.

This room has a variety of levels and equipment to develop small and large muscle development. It also provides for group interaction as well as individual pursuits.

Change the room arrangement to add variety to the curriculum. For example, put the block area closer to the sand box and the car unit near the loft to expand sociodramatic play. Move the room divider to create different paths or to block off an area that is not being used.

If lunches or snacks are served in the room, the science table, writing table and the table in the middle can be pulled out to accommodate this. If another exit is necessary for fire requirements, it could be located left of the loft.

# Designing Effective Early Childhood Environments

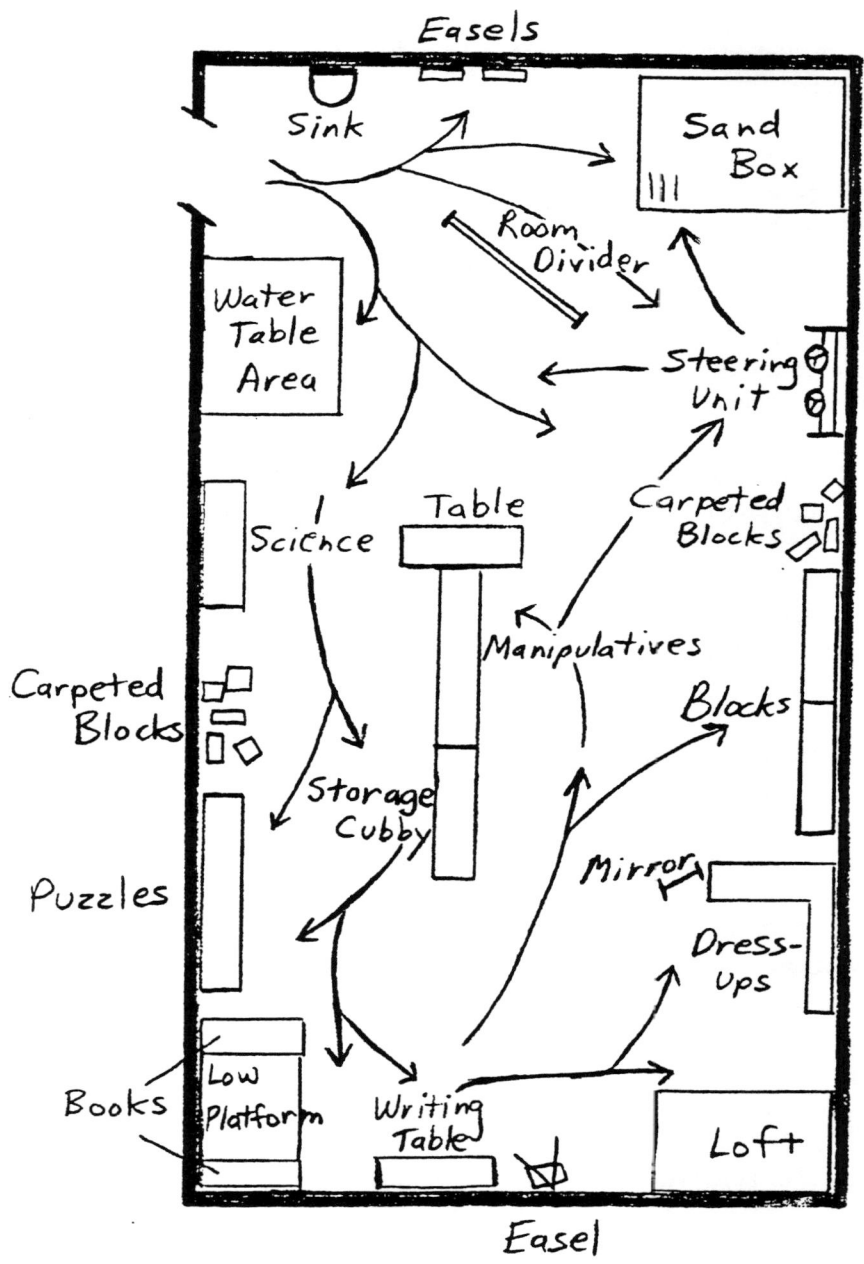

Figure 1

## Chapter 5: Suggested Equipment for Early Childhood Environments

**Figure 2** shows a room with more restricted space than Figure 1. The room divider keeps children from dumping materials in the center of the room and softens the squared or rectangular appearance of the room. This structure also assists in directing children to specific areas.

The arrangement encourages the combination of block, sociodramatic and manipulatives areas. The other half of the room is designated for individual learning. The two tables shown in the diagram are used for learning centers, art activities, snacks or lunch.

Because of the space limitations in the room, large muscle activities take place in another area of the building. (A water source should also be near the room.)

**Figure 3** displays an arrangement enabling the teacher to store extra equipment and materials in the room. The storage units take up the least amount of space. This room arrangement allows for movement in the middle and the open traffic pattern prohibits congestions.

The round and writing tables are used for art, snacks and lunch. To save space in the housekeeping corner, hooks are attached to the back of the manipulative shelf for dress up clothes.

This arrangement allows for ample floor space, and the open traffic pattern gives the teacher a complete view of the room. The manipulative shelf creates a definite boundary to separate the manipulatives from the housekeeping area. Though the manipulatives and house need to be separate, the house easily flows into the block area to further dramatic play. The shelf tops are good for the drying of wet art creations.

**Figure 4** gives a three-dimensional look to the block/construction area and suggests activities which can be carried out close by. The raised platform gives more space and possibilities for a variety of building activities. Blocks are used in front of the shelves or on and under the platform. The blocks overlap with the housekeeping area if it is located nearby, and manipulatives for fine motor development expand the play activities.

**Figure 5** suggests a layout for a water table/art area. For the young child, the water table is inviting and is effective at the beginning of the year to entice the child into the classroom. While at the water table, activities in the rest of the room can be viewed. Obviously, floor surfaces are washable and a boundary is defined to keep the contents away from the doorway.

An arrangement for a sociodramatic area is suggested in **Figure 6**. The loft is used as a starting point for basic themes in sociodramatic play. Props are inside the structure, but can overflow to the dress up area and a table or two. The room divider allows traffic to flow in and out, but also creates a boundary for this area. A few changes include removing the round table and replacing it with the car unit or a tent

Designing Effective Early Childhood Environments

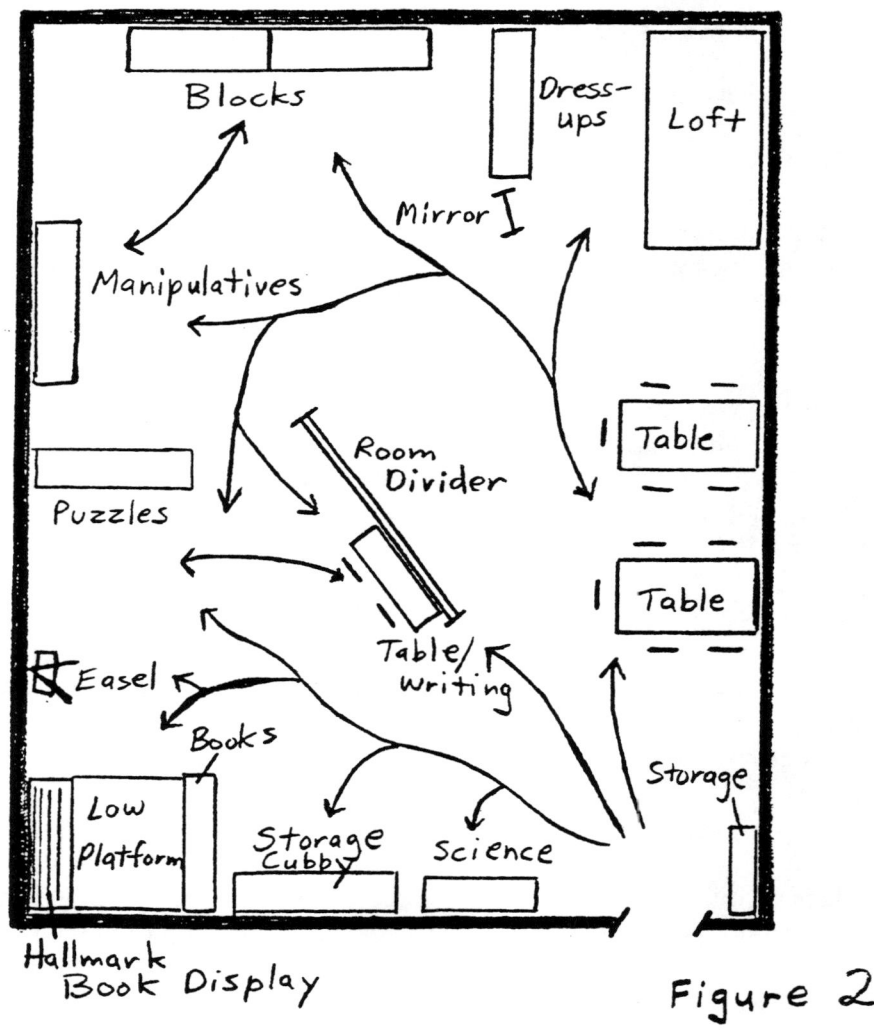

Figure 2

Chapter 5: Suggested Equipment for Early Childhood Environments

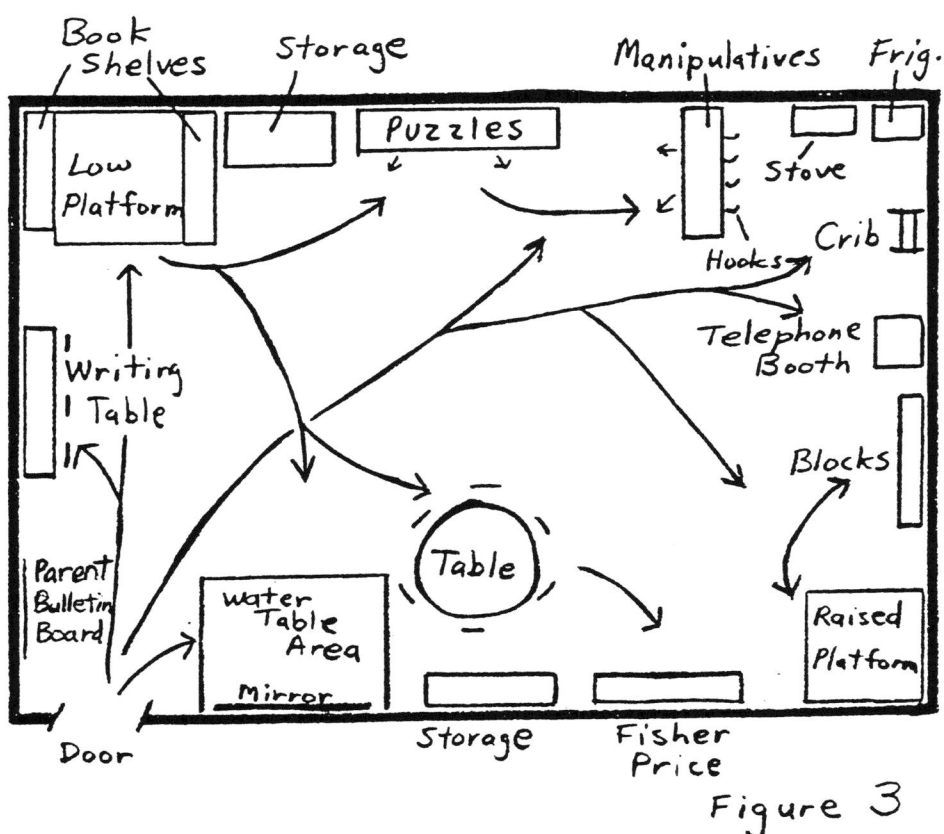

Figure 3

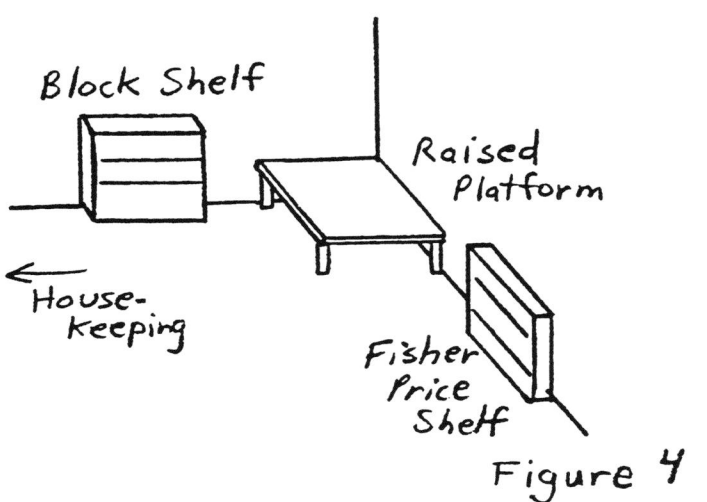

Figure 4

Designing Effective Early Childhood Environments

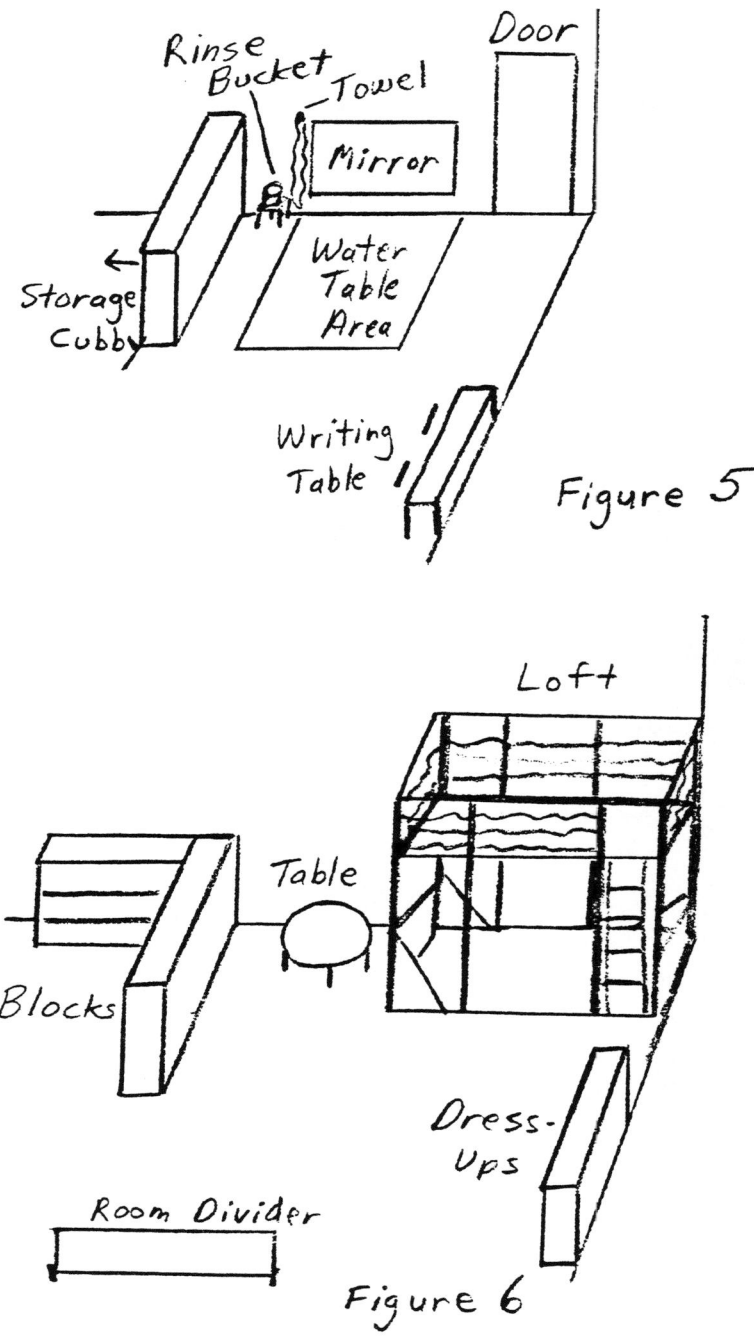

Figure 5

Figure 6

## Chapter 5: Suggested Equipment for Early Childhood Environments

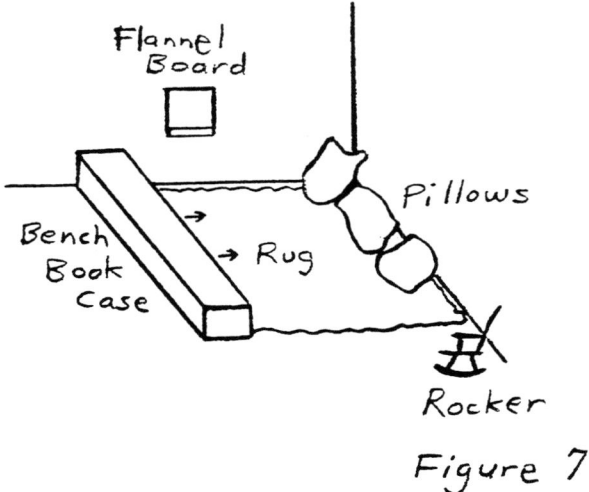

Figure 7

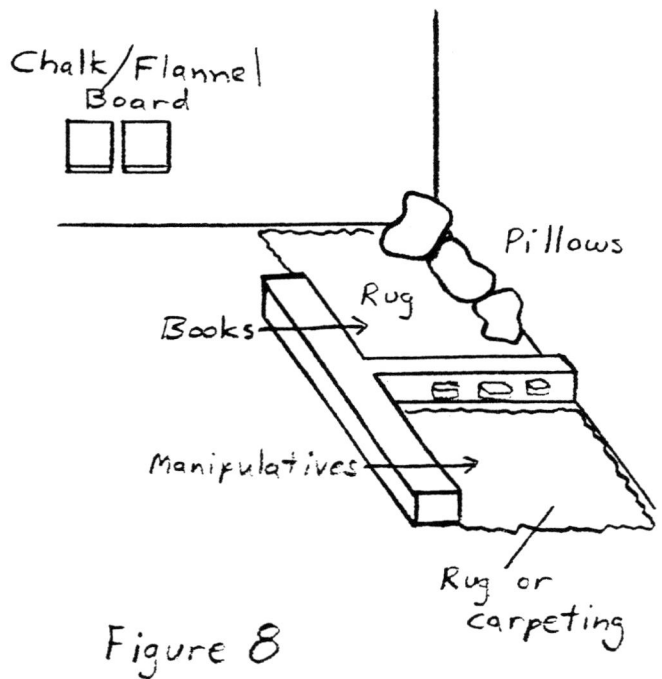

Figure 8

## Designing Effective Early Childhood Environments

or a campfire scene.

**Figures 7 through 10** are suggestions for quiet areas. Some of these figures show bench-like bookcases. The flannel board in **Figure 7** is used to re-enact stories or nursery rhymes. The carpeted blocks are next to the bookcases, outside the reading areas to serve as little stools. Children create their own reading/desk area or writing area when carpeted stool is placed next to the bench/bookcase.

In **Figure 8** the chalk/flannel boards could be an extension of the reading or writing area located to the left of the easels. For young children who like to find crawl spaces to work in, the manipulative area provides crawling spaces filled with finger toys. These areas are carpeted because the children are on the floor. If the benches are wide enough (15 to 18 inches), locked storage areas for extra books, puzzles, manipulatives, games, paper and writing utensils is built on the opposite side from the materials.

**Figure 9** shows a reading area with more privacy. Pictures on the wall at the child's eye level are an invitation to enter the area.

The arrangement in **Figure 10** allows for a variety of movement. The raised platform is available for puzzle constructions or for crawling into a place to be alone. Also, if near a window, the children look outside from a sturdy surface. Book browsing occurs on or under the raised platform. The puzzles are worked on the platform or on the floor in front of the shelf unit. The book area is defined with the use of a low platform and shelves on both sides. The room divider helps direct traffic into and out of these areas and keeps the puzzles and books separated.

These sample arrangements are only suggestions for teachers and administrators. Sometimes only parts of these can be used and other times they can be expanded upon. When rearranging the room or an area, make the changes slowly. Before making any changes, first, collect data on the number of children and frequency of activity in each area, then decide what ONE area to target and only change one thing at a time so the effects can be documented. Assess the consequences of the change and proceed with more changes if necessary. After each change, evaluate the children's activities before and after the change.

Chapter 5: Suggested Equipment for Early Childhood Environments

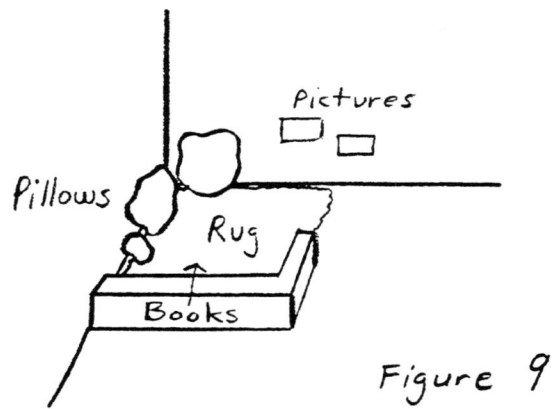

Figure 9

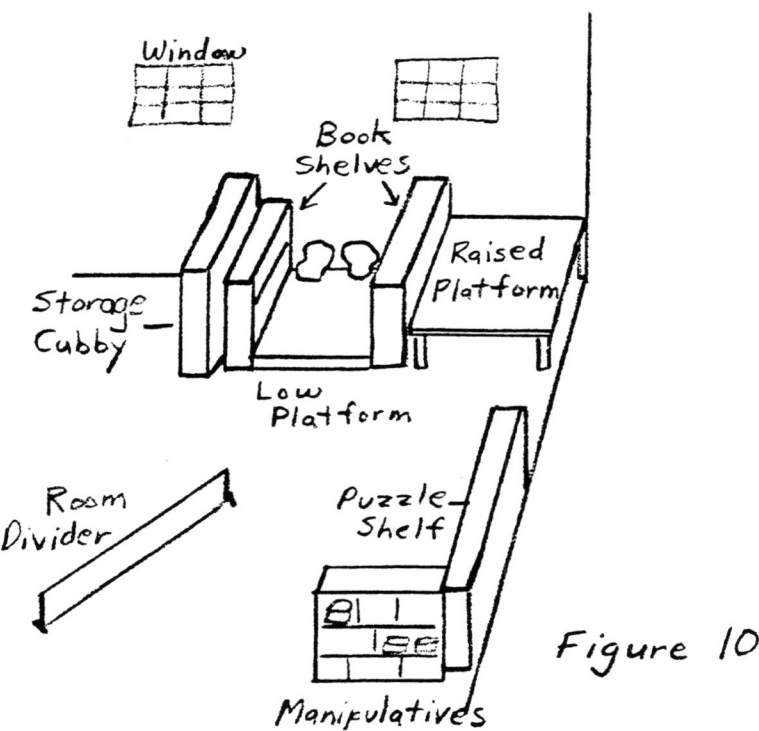

Figure 10

# Designing Effective Early Childhood Environments

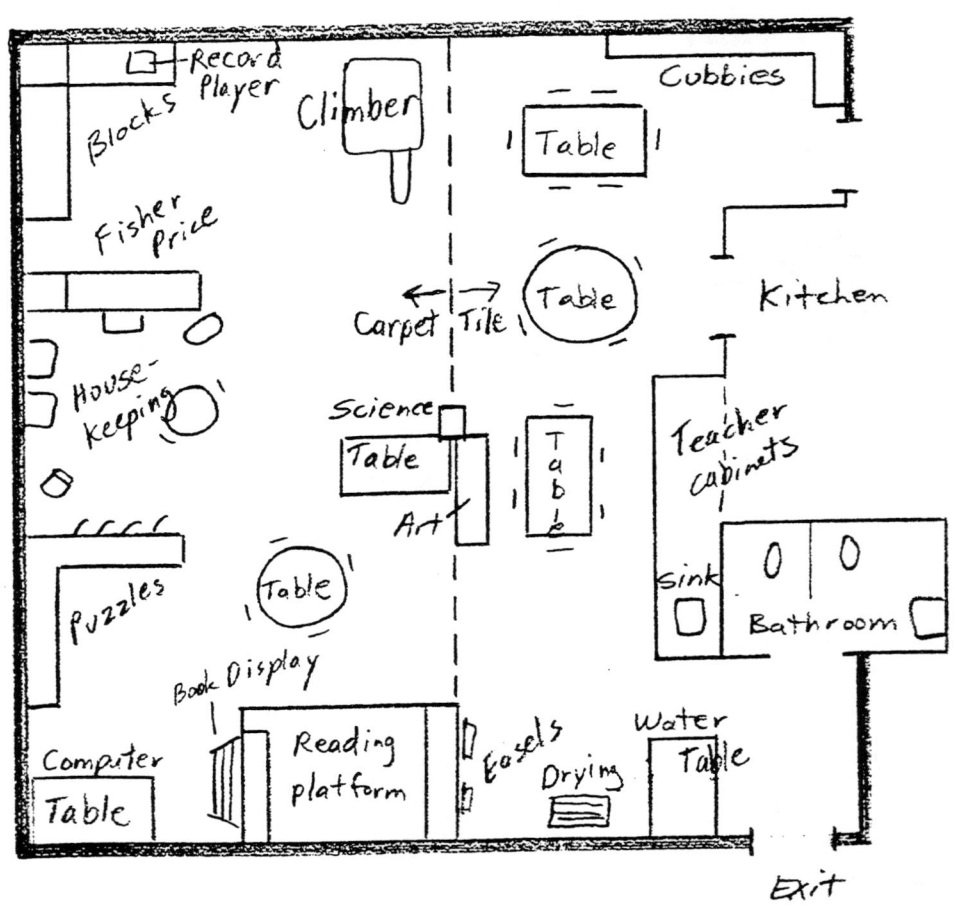

Chapter 5: Suggested Equipment for Early Childhood Environments

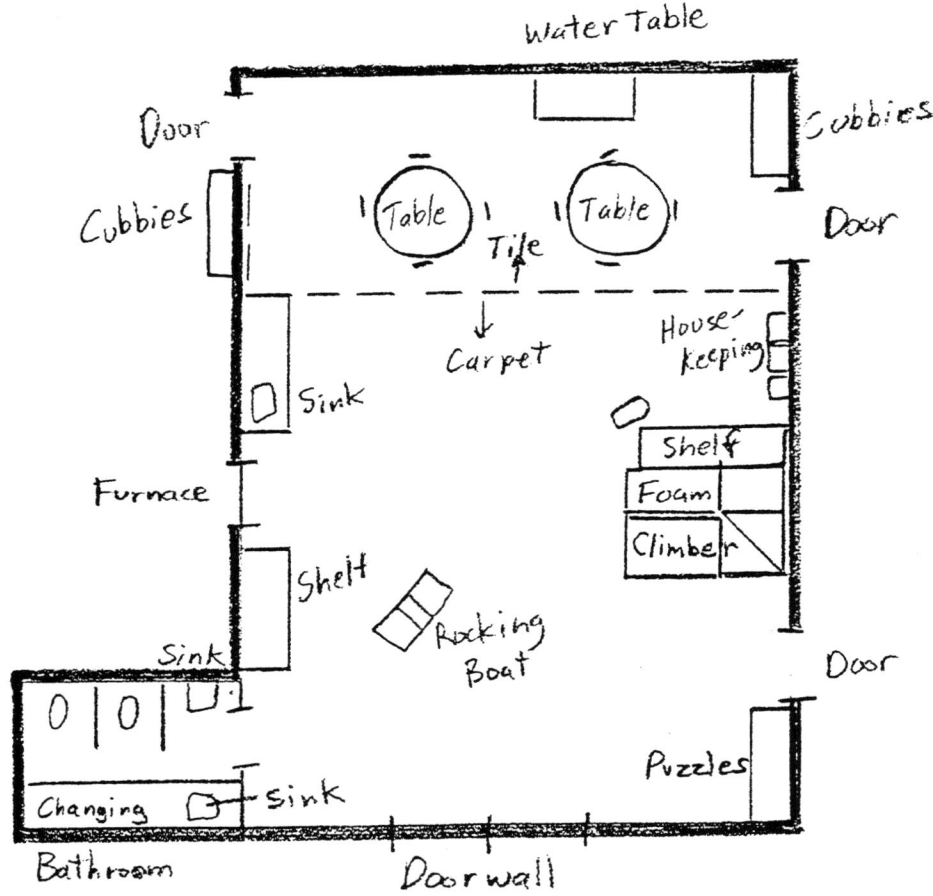

# Room Arrangements for Primary Grades

The following room arrangements are suggested for use in primary grade classrooms. These rooms almost always include desks or tables so each child has a work space. Unfortunately, these pieces of equipment often dominate the classroom and children are confined to their desks for long periods of time. These suggestions provide for room arrangements which would facilitate the following of guidelines (Iowa 1990) which state that no more than one third of the day should be spent by young children at a desk.

Primary grade classrooms are divided into four general areas: those designated for (1) exploratory learning, (2) cooperative learning, (3) small group learning, and (4) large group learning. Within the area designed for exploratory learning, children may work by themselves, with a partner, or in a small group. These combinations of social interaction are all happening simultaneously.

The cooperative learning area needs to be flexible so it is large enough for the entire class to participate in small cooperative groups at once, or allow for a group of two children to work cooperatively on a project while others are working independently at their desks/tables.

A teacher often works with small groups of children on various tasks and thus a small group learning area is needed.

Provision is also made for a large group learning area which would contain the desks/tables, but are cleared so children use it for sitting on the floor for a discussion, movement activities, project work and creative drama.

Organization of the space in the classroom is based on either grouping of children, e.g. individual, small group, large group, or purpose of the activity, e.g. exploration, cooperation, discussion, sharing of information, etc. Often there will be overlap between these.

**Exploratory Learning**

Materials described in an earlier part of this book in primary grade classrooms include the draftsman's easel, block shelves, manipulative shelves, puzzle shelf, felt/flannel easel, and bean bag toss. Centers facilitating exploratory learning are content based and include math and science centers, all with manipulatives. The side by side easels allow for exploration of art media as well as provide a vehicle for integrating writing. These centers and/or the materials described are often placed around the walls of the classroom and in the corners. Children are able to move from their desks/tables to the various areas easily and without disruption of others.

## Cooperative Learning

All of the materials are used by children working in a cooperative goal structure as long as the size of the group was appropriate to the amount of equipment available. An art area which would provide children with materials for construction of a planned project and an opportunity to foster cooperative interactions among children. The center is designed for cooperative learning and the groups' membership fluctuates depending on the interest of the children.

Other centers planned for cooperative interaction are the writing and unit centers. In the writing center, various writing implements (markers, pencils, crayons, pens) are placed in containers such as boxes or coffee cans which have been covered so no sharp edges are exposed. Lined as well as plain paper is available. The paper is bound into small books for children's use. File cards, envelopes, pads of paper and colored construction paper are kept on shelves nearby. Tools such as a paper punch, staples and stapler, stamps and stamp pads, compass and protractor should also be accessible.

The unit center houses materials children have brought from home. Blocks and 1" x 6" boards are used to build shelves to keep the materials on and children spend a lot of time discussing these items in small cooperative groups.

## Small Group

Primary grade teachers work with children individually and in small groups. Small group areas are located on the raised platform, or on the upper level of the loft or in the lower level of the loft. A room divider is used to form other areas for use by small groups such as stations where tape recorders, computers, cameras and headphones are found.

## Summary

In the primary grade classroom, it is important for the teacher to realize children at this age need to have a classroom designed to encourage movement and talking and to direct their own learning. The environment resembles a preschool/kindergarten more than a junior high or high school. Areas are intriguing and draw children to them. There are nooks and crannies where children go to be alone. Small group and large group areas are flexible. Carpet the room to encourage children to be on the floor. Large cushions or carpeted blocks should always be available for children to use. And finally, the children should be allowed to suggest arrangement ideas and create and care for the environment with the teacher. This is their home away from home.

# Designing Effective Early Childhood Environments

Photo copyright April S. Haase

Chapter 5: Suggested Equipment for Early Childhood Environments

Photo copyright April S. Haase

Designing Effective Early Childhood Environments

Photo copyright April S. Haase

# Appendices

- **Bibliography**
- **Resource Books**
- **Resource Publications**
- **Resource Organizations**

# BIBLIOGRAPHY

Acredolo, L.P., Pick, H.L., & Olsen, M.G. (1975). Environmental differentiation and familiarity as determinants of children's memory for spatial location. *Developmental Psychology,* 11, 495-501.

Allen, A. & Neterer, E. (1974). A guide to play materials. *Play: Children's Business*, pp. 50-59.

Ames, L. & Ilg, F. (1976). *Your four year old.* New York: Delacorte.

Ames, L. & Ilg, F. (1976). *Your three year old.* New York: Delacorte.

Ames, L. & Ilg, F. (1981). *Your five year old.* New York: Delacorte.

Appelbaum, M.M., Day, D.E., & Olds, A.R. (1984). Fine details: Organizing and displaying materials. *Beginnings Magazine*, pp. 13-16.

Blake, O.W. (1968). What every child needs from physical education. *Physical education for children's healthful living,* pp. 9-12. Washington, DC: Association for Childhood Education International.

Blatz, W. E., M.B., & Bott, H. (1930). *The management of young children.* New York: William Morrow.

Brault, D. (1968). Environment for learning: Classroom, gymnasium, and playground. *Physical education for children's healthful living,* (pp. 55-62). Washington, DC: Association for Childhood Educational International.

Bredekamp, S. (Ed.). (1986). *Developmentally appropriate practice.* Washington, D.C.: National Association for Education of Young Children.

Butler, A. L., Gotts, E. E., & Quisenberry, N. L. (1978). *Play as development.* Columbus: Charles E. Merrill.

Canter, D. (1977). *The psychology of place.* London: Architectural Press.

Cohen, S. & Lesak, A. (1977). *Environment and Behavior*, 9 (4), 559-572.

Cook, M. B. (1967). *The come-alive classroom: Practical projects for elementary teachers.* J. H. Caldwell & L. J. Christiansen (Eds.). West Nyac, NY: Parker.

Cratty, B. J. (1973). *Teaching motor skills.* New Jersey: Prentice Hall.

Dale, E. (1972). *Building a learning environment.* Bloomington, IN: Phi Delta Kappa.

Day, D. E. & Sheehan, R. (1974). Elements of a better preschool. *Young Children, 30,* pp. 15-23.

Doke, L. A. & Risley, T. R. (1972). The organization of day care environments: Required vs. optional activities. *Journal of Applied Behavior Analysis, 5,* pp. 405-420.

Elder, J. L. & Pederson, D. R. (1978). Preschool children's use of objects in symbolic play. *Child Development, 49,* pp. 500-504.

Evans, E. B., Saia, G., & Evans, E. A. (1974). *Designing a day care center.* Boston: Beacon Press.

Federlein, A.C. (1989). *The Business of Child Care.* Dubuque, IA: Kendall Hunt Publishers.

Field, T., De Stefano, L. & Koewler, J. H. (1982). Fantasy play of toddlers and preschoolers. *Developmental Psychology, 18,* pp. 503-508.

Fleming, R. S. (1968). Movement--an essential in a good school day. *Physical education for children's healthful living,* (pp. 13-20). Washington DC: Association for Childhood Education International.

Foremean, G. & Hill, F. (1980). *Constructive play: Applying Piaget in the preschool.* Monterey, CA: Brooks/Cole.

Forte, I. & Mackenzie, J. (1978). *Nooks, crannies and corners: Learning centers for creative classrooms.* Nashville, TN: Incentive Publications.

Friedman, E. (1973). Play is serious business. *Play Scapes,* pp. 12-16.

Fromberg, D. P. (1977). *Early childhood education: A perceptual models curriculum.* New York: John Wiley & Sons.

Frost, J. L. & Klein, B. L. (1983). *Children's play and playgrounds.* Austin, TX: Playscapes International.

Frostig, M. (1970). *Movement education: Theory and practice.* Chicago: Follett.

Gandini, L. (1984). Not just anywhere: Making child care centers into "particular" places. *Beginnings Magazine,* pp. 17-20.

*Gift of Time.* (1982). New Haven, CN: Gesell Institute of Human Development.

Gramza, A. F., Corush, J., & Ellis, M. J. (1972). Children's play on trestles differing in complexity: A study of play equipment design. *Journal of Leisure Research, 4,* pp. 303-311.

Greenberg, P. (1979). Lucy Sprague Mitchell: A major missing link between early childhood education in the 1890's-1930's. *Young Children, 42,* pp. 70-84.

Hanson, M. R. (1968). *Physical Education for Children's Healthful Living,* pp. 71-76. Washington, DC: Association for Childhood Education International.

Hartwig, H. (1968). Safety education--important facet of physical education. *Physical Education for Children's Healthful Living,* pp. 49-54. Washington, DC: Association for Childhood Education International.

Hazen, N. L., Lockman, J. J., & Pick, H. L. (1978). The development of children's representations of large-scale environments. *Child Development, 49,* pp. 623-636.

Headley, N. E. & Liddle, E. A. (1974). Environmental opportunities for creative-exploratory play. *Play: Children's Business,* pp. 20-27.

Hirsch, E. S. (Ed.). (1974). *The block book.* Washington, DC: National Association for the Education of Young Children.

Holloway, G. E. (1967). *An introduction to the child's conception of space.* London: Routledge & Kegan Paul.

Johnson, J. E. & Ershler, J. (1981). Developmental trends in preschool play as a function of classroom program and child gender. *Child Development, 52,* pp. 995-1004.

Kephart, N. E. (1975). Perceptual-motor problems of children. In S. A. Kirk & J. McCarthy (Eds.). *Learning Disabilities.* Selected ACLD Papers. pp. 16-22. Boston: Houghton Mifflin.

Kritchevsky, S. & Prescott, E., with L. Walling. (1977). *Planning environments for young children: Physical space.* Washington, DC: National Association for the Education of Young Children.

Lerch, H. A., Becker, J. E., Ward, B. M., & Nelson, J. A. (1974). *Perceptual-motor learning-theory and practice.* Palo Alto, CA: Peek Publications.

Lewin, K. (1931). Environmental forces in child behavior and development. In C. Murchison (Ed.). *A handbook of child psychology.* Worcester, MA: Clark University.

Loo, C. M. (1972). The effects of spatial density on the social behavior of children. *Journal of Applied Social Psychology, 2,* pp. 372-381.

Loughlin, C. E. & Suina, J. H. (1982). *The learning environment: An instructional strategy.* New York: Teachers College Press.

Lovell, K. (1961). *The growth of basic mathematical and scientific concepts in children.* New York: Philosophical Library.

Mante, D. R. & Mathisen, B. W. (1977). *How to develop a model school and model classrooms for young children.* Redwood City, CA: Educational Publications.

Mason, J. (1982). *The environment of play.* West Point, NY: Leisure Press.

McGrew, P. L. (1970). Social and spatial density effects on spacing behavior in preschool children. *Journal of Child Psychology and Allied Disciplines, 11,* pp. 197-205.

Omwake, E. B. (1984). The young child...We know so much--we know so little. In G. Engstrom (Ed.) *The significance of the young child's motor development,* pp. 10-15. Washington, DC: National Association for the Education of Young Children.

Osmon, F. L. (1973). *Patterns for designing children's centers.* New York: Educational Facilities Laboratories.

Packard, R. C. (1972). *The hidden image.* Notre Dame, IN: Fides Publishing.

Pollowy, A. M. (1974). The child in the physical environment: A design problem. In G. Coates (Ed.) *Alternative learning environments,* pp. 370-381. Stroudsburg, PA: Dowden, Hutchinson & Ross.

Prescott, E. (1984). When you think about spaces. *Beginnings,* pp. 3-5.

Propst, R. (1975). Human needs and working places. In T. G. David & B. D. Wright (Eds.) *Learning environments,* pp. 89-90. Chicago: University of Chicago Press.

Prohansky, E. & Wolfe, M. (1975). The physical setting and open education. In T. G. David & B. D. Wright (Eds.), *Learning environments,* pp. 31-48. Chicago: University of Chicago Press.

Provenzo, E. F., Jr., & Brett, A. (1983). *The complete block book.* Syracuse, NY: Syracuse University Press.

Rasmus, C. J. (1968). A formula for play: Child + space + imagination. *Physical education for children's healthful living,* pp. 27-36. Washington, DC: Association for Childhood Education International.

Robison, H. F. (1977). *Exploring teaching in early childhood education.* Boston: Allyn & Bacon.

Rubin, K. H. (1977, September). Play behaviors of young children. *Young Children,* 32, pp. 16-24.

Rudolph, M. (1973). *From hand to head: A handbook for teachers of pre-school programs.* New York: Webster Division, McGraw-Hill.

Sava, S. G. (1975). *Learning through discovery for young children.* New York: McGraw-Hill.

Schickedanz, J. A., York, M. E., Stewart, I. S., & White, D. (1977). *Strategies for teaching young children.* Englewood Cliffs, NJ: Prentice-Hall.

Seiderman, A. S. (1972). *A look at perceptual-motor training.* Academic Therapy, 7, pp. 315-321.

Shapiro, S. (1975). Preschool ecology: A study of three environmental variables. *Reading Improvements,* 12, pp. 236-241.

Sheehan, R. & Day, D. E. (1975). Is open space just empty space? *Day Care and Early Education, 3,* pp. 10-13, 47.

Shipley, F. & Carpenter, E. (1962). *Freedom to move.* Washington, DC: National Education Association Department of Elementary-Kindergarten-Nursery Education.

Spodek, B. (1985). *Teaching in the early years.* Englewood Cliffs, NJ: Prentice-Hall.

Sponseller, D. (Ed.). (1974). *Play as learning medium.* Washington, DC: National Association for the Education of Young Children.

Stevens, J. H., Jr., & King, E. W. (1976). *Administering early childhood education programs*. Boston: Little, Brown.

Sylva, K., Brunner, J. S., & Genova, P. (1976). The role of play in the problem solving of children 3-5 years old. *Play--its role in development and evolution,* pp. 244-257. New York: Basic Books.

Taylor, A. P. & Vlastos, G. (1975). *School zone: Learning environments for children.* New York: Van Nostrand Reinhold.

Trencher, B. R. (1976). *Child's play: An activities and materials handbook.* Atlanta: Humanics Limited.

Van Alstyne, D., Ph.D. (1932). *Play behavior and choice of play materials of preschool children.* Chicago: University of Chicago Press.

Vergeront, J. (1987). *Places and spaces for preschool and primary (indoors).* Washington, DC: National Association for the Education of Young Children.

Wadsworth, B. J. (1971). *Piaget's theory of cognitive development.* New York: Longman.

Werner, P. H. & Burton, E. C. (1979). *Learning through movement.* St. Louis: C. V. Mosby.

Whitehurst, K. E. (1984). What movement means to him. In G. Engstrom (Ed.), *The significance of the young child's motor development* pp. 51-55. Washington, DC: National Association for the Education of Young Children.

Ziemer, M. (1987). Science and the early childhood curriculum: One thing leads to another. *Young Children, 42,* pp. 44-51.

Zifferblatt, S. M. (1972). Architecture and human behavior: Toward increased understanding of a functional relationship. *Educational Technology, 12,* pp. 54-57.

Zion, L. C. & Raker, B. L. (1986). *The physical side of thinking.* Springfield, IL: Charles C. Thomas.

# RESOURCES

The following books and journals are suggestions for additional ideas in designing a creative classroom, including evaluation and arrangements of equipment. Outdoor materials and arrangements are also discussed.

D'Eugenio, T. (1971). *Building with tires*. Cambridge, MA: Early Childhood Education Study of Advisory for Open Education.

Engel, B. s. (1973). *Arranging the informal classroom*. Newton, MA: Education Development Center.

Harms, T. (1970). *Evaluating settings for learning*. Young Children, 25, pp. 304-308.

Hogan, P. (1982). *The nuts and bolts of playground construction*. West Point, NY: Leisure Press.

Ledford, B. R. (1981). Interior design: Impact on learning achievement. In P. J. Sleeman & D. M. Rockwell (Eds.), *Designing Learning Environments*. New York: Longman.

Loughlin, C. (1978). Arranging the learning environment. *Insights, 11*, pp. 2-5.

Yamamoto, K. (Ed.). (1979). *Children in time and space*. New York: College Press.

Yardley, A. (1974). *Structure in early learning*. London: Evans Brothers.

Appendices

# PUBLICATION RESOURCES

**National Newsletters**

*Child Care Information Exchange*, Exchange Press, P.O. Box 2890, Redmond, WA 98073

*Child Care Resources*, Child Care Fair, P.O. Box 324, Mound, MN 55364

*Early Years,* Allen Raymound, Inc., 11 Hale Lane, Box 1266, Darien, CT 06820

*Education USA*, National School Public Relations Associations, 1501 Lee Highway, Suite 201, Arlington, VA 22209

*ERIC Digest and Annotated Resource Lists*, ERIC Clearinghouse on Elementary and Early Childhood Education, University of Illinois, College of Education, 805 West Pennsylvania, Urbana, IL 61801

*First Teacher*, First Teacher, Inc., Box 29, Bridgeport, CT 06602

*Family Day Care Exchange*, Cooperative Extension Service, Publications Distribution, Iowa State University, Ames, IA 50011

*Family Day Care Bulletin*, The Children's Foundation, 815 Fifteenth, Suite 928, Washington, DC 20005

*Report on Preschool Programs*, 951 Pershing, Silver Spring, MD 20910-4464

*Parent and Preschooler Newsletter*, P.O. Box 1851, Garden City, NY 11530

*PARENT-ing*, Cleveland Publications, 194 Strand, Coloma, MI 49038

*School Age Notes*, P.O. Box 120674, Nashville, TN 37212

*Totline*, Totline Press, P.O. Box 2255, Everett, WA 98203

**Periodicals**

*Child Care Quarterly*, Human Sciences Press, Inc. 72 Fifth Avenue, New

York, NY 10011

*Child Development*, Society for Research in Child Development, Inc. University of Chicago Press, 5801 South Ellis, Chicago, Il 60637

*Childhood Education*, Association for Childhood Education International, 11141 Georgia, Suite 200, Wheaton, MD 20902

*Day Care and Early Education Magazine*, Day care and Child Development Council of America, Inc., Human Sciences Press, Inc., 72 Fifth Avenue, New York, NY 1001

*Early Childhood Research Quarterly*, ERIC Clearinghouse on Elementary and Early Childhood Educationand Natinal Association for the Education of Young Children, Ablex Publishers, 355 Chestnut, Norwood, NJ 07648

*Exceptional Children*, Council for Exceptional Children, 1920 Association Drive, Reston, VA 22091

*The Instructor*, Instructor Publications, Inc., 545 Fifth Avenue, New York, NY 10017

*Journal of Research in Childhood Education*, Association for Childhood Education International, 11141 Georgia, Suite 200, Wheaton, MC 20902

*Language Arts*, National Council of Teachers of English, 1111 Kenyon, Urbana, IL 61801

*Science and Children*, National Science Teachers Association, 1742 Connecticut NW, Washington DC 20009

*Young Children*, National Assocation for the Education of Young Children, 1834 Connecticut NW, Washington, DC 20009

## Catalogs

National Association for the Education of Young Children (NAEYC) Early Childhood Catalog, NAEYC Affiliate Services, 1834 Connecticut NW, Washington, DC 2009

The National Directory of Child Care Resource and Referral Agencies, California Child Care Resource and Referral Network, 809 Lincoln Way, San Francisco, CA 94122

The Olive Press, Multi-Cultural Resources for Teaching Young Children, 5727 Dunmore, West Bloomfield, MI 48322-1613

Appendices

# RESOURCE ORGANIZATIONS

AIDS Action Council, 729 Eighth SE, Suite 200, Washington, D.C. 20003

AIDS Resource Center, National Parent Teacher Association, 700 North Rush, Chicago, IL 60611-2571

American Academy of Pediatrics, 141 Northwest Point, Elk Grove Village, IL 60009

American Association of Psychiatric Services for Children, 1001 Connecticut NW, Suite 800, Washington, D.C. 20036

American Child Care Services, P.O. Box 548, 532 Settlers Landing Road, Hampton, VA 23669

Association for Childhood Education International, 11141 Georgia Avenue, Suite 200, Wheaton, MD 20902

American Montessori Society, 175 Fifth Avenue, New York, NY 10010

American Red Cross, AIDS Education Office, 1730 D Street NW, Washington, DC 20006

Catalyst, 250 Park Avenue South, New York, NY 1003-1459

Child Care Action Campaign, 99 Hudson, Suite 1233, New York, NY 10013

Community Coordinated Child Care of Central Florida, Inc., 1612 East Colonial Drive, Orlando, FL 32803

Child Care Law Center, 624 Market, Suite 815, San Francisco, CA 94105

Child Development Associates National Credentialing Program, 1341 G Street NW, Suite 8202, Washington, DC 20005

Children's Foundation, 815 Fifteenth, Suite 926, Washington, DC 20005

Center for Public Advocacy Research, Inc., 12 West Thirty Seventh, New York, NY 10018

Child Welfare League of America, Inc., 67 Irving Place, New York, NY 10010

Children's Book Council, 67 Irving Place, New York, NY 10010

Children's Defense Fund, 122 C Street NW, Washington, DC 20001

Council for Exceptional Children, 1920 Association Drive, Reston, VA 22091

Council for Early Childhood Professional Recognition, 1718 Connecticut NW, Washington, DC 20009

Council on Interracial Books for Children, 1841 Broadway, Room 500, New York, NY 10023

Danjo, Inc. Computer Programs, P.O. Box 380713, San Antonio, TX 78280

Department of Health and Human Services, Public Health Service, Centers for Disease Control, Atlanta, GA 30333

Education Development Center, 55 Chapel Street, Newton, MA 02160

ERIC Clearinghouse in Elementary and Early Childhood Education, University of Illinois, 805 West Pennsylvania Avenue, Urbana, IL 61801

High/Scope Educational Research Foundation, 600 North River, Ypsilanti, MI 48198-2989

Hispanic AIDS Forum, 853 Broadway, Suite 2007, New York, NY 10003

Home and School Institute, Special Projects Office, 1201 Sixteenth NW, Washington, DC 20036

Institute for Childhood Resources, 1169 Howard Street, San Francisco, CA 94103

Institute for Responsive Education, Don Davies, 605 Commonwealth, Boston, MA 02215

International Reading Association, 800 Barksdale Road, P.O. Box 8139, Newark, DE 19714

Los Angeles AIDS Project, 7362 Santa Monica, Los Angeles, CA 90046

Appendices

National Association for the Education of Young Children, 1834 Connecticut, NW, Washington, DC 20009

National Association for Gifted Children, 5100 North Edgewood, St. Paul, MN 55112

National Association of State Boards of Education, 701 North Fairfax, Suite 340, Alexandria, VA 22314

National Black Child Development Institute, Inc. 1463 Rhode Island NW, Washington, DC 20005

National Committee for Citizens in Education, 10840 Little Patuxent Parkway, Suite 301, Columbia, ND 21044

National Conference of State Legislatures, 1050 Seventeenth, Suite 200, Denver, CO 80265

National Education Association, 1201 Sixteenth NW, Washington, DC 20036

National School Boards Association, 1680 Duke, Alexandria, VA 22314

National School Public Relations Association, 1501 Lee Highway, Suite 201, Arlington, VA 22209

National Parent Teacher Association, 700 North Rush, Chicago, IL 60611

Resources for Child Caring, 906 North Dale, St. Paul, MN 55103

Save the Children Child Care Support Center, 1340 Spring NW, Suite 200, Atlanta, GA 30309

School Age Child Care Project, Wellesley College, Center for Research on Women, Wellesley, MA 02161

Society for Research in Child Development, University of Chicago Press, 5801 Ellis, Chicago, IL 60637

Southern Association on Children Under Six, Box 5403 Brady Station, Little Rock, AR 72215

World Organization of Early Childhood Education, U.S. National Committee, Box 931, Fresno, CA 93714

Work/Family Directions, 16 Galen, Watertown, MA 02172

Work and Family Information Center, The Conference Board, 845 Third, New York, NY 10022

Designing Effective Early Childhood Environments

Photo copyright April S. Haase